12.30.72

IBSEN AND HIS CREATION

By the Same Author

Dostoevsky and his Creation

(Collins, 7s. 6d.)

∵

Some Press Opinions

'It is an able piece of work. . . . Certainly Mr Lavrin gets nearer to a clear picture of Dostoevsky's mental struggles, which are so apparent in every page of his novels, than any other writer we have yet come across.'—*Times Lit. Supp.*

'The nearest approach to a sane estimate of Dostoevsky.' —*Manchester Guardian.*

'M. Janko Lavrin has written a book which, in its penetrating illumination, deserves to stand beside Merejkowski's great *Tolstoi and Dostoevsky*. Here is interpretative criticism of the kind that sends one, hot-footed, back to the novels.'— *Time and Tide.*

'After having ploughed through the too arid wastes of the analysers, it is most refreshing to meet such a book as Mr Lavrin's, a book that gives us a synthetic picture of Dostoevsky and the Russia of his time.'—*The New Age.*

'Mr Lavrin's work is the best appreciation of Dostoevsky that has yet appeared in the English language.'—*The Glasgow Herald.*

'The whole is a truly masterly work of profound criticism.' —*The Country Life.*

IBSEN
AND HIS CREATION
A PSYCHO-CRITICAL STUDY
by JANKO LAVRIN

Author of 'DOSTOEVSKY AND HIS CREATION'

HASKELL HOUSE PUBLISHERS LTD.

Publishers of Scarce Scholarly Books

NEW YORK, N. Y. 10012

1972

HASKELL HOUSE PUBLISHERS Ltd.

Publishers of Scarce Scholarly Books

280 LAFAYETTE STREET

NEW YORK. N. Y. 10012

Library of Congress Cataloging in Publication Data

Lavrin, Janko, 1887–
    Ibsen and his creation.

    I. Ibsen, Henrik, 1828–1906. II. Title.
PT8895.L3 1972   839.8'2'26   72–2140
ISBN 0-8383-1484-8

Printed in the United States of America

1736157

TO EDWARD MOORE

NOTE

THIS book is an attempt to deal, above all, with Ibsen as representative of modern consciousness. In this respect it may be considered a complement to the merely æsthetic or merely social criticisms of Ibsen and his works. Although the present study forms an independent whole, it is nevertheless inwardly connected with my psycho-critical study of Dostoevsky (*Dostoevsky and his Creation*, Collins) and also with two other studies which are to follow.

The quotations from plays have been taken mainly from the excellent English edition of Ibsen's works arranged by William Archer (Heinemann). For extracts from letters I am indebted to Hodder & Stoughton's *Ibsen's Correspondence*, and for those from speeches to *Speeches and Letters of Ibsen* (Frank Palmer).

The substance of this work appeared originally in the *New Age*, and I wish to express my sincere thanks to the Editor for permission to re-publish it.

J. L.

CONTENTS

CHAPTER I
Ibsen's Dramas and the Drama of Ibsen

I

IBSEN'S DRAMAS AND THE DRAMA OF IBSEN

I

ART is a symbolical diary of mankind's inner evolution. The history of art is the history of mankind's soul, for each epoch bequeaths its soul to future generations mainly through its art. An artistic creator is thus the best witness for his own time. He is highly 'contemporary,' in so far as the soul of his time finds in him its most intense, its synthetic, expression. But the more he feels the secret pulse of his era the greater is the burden he has to sustain—since every one who is profoundly sensitive to his own epoch is for this very reason spiritually also in advance of it, and, therefore, usually suffers from it, judges it, and, in some way or other, reacts against it. Hence, the importance of an artist's individual attitude towards the vital values of his epoch. This conscious or unconscious attitude determines, as a rule, his choice of subjects, his manner of treating them, and

—above all—the inner significance of his art.

It is just at this point that Art is frequently misunderstood and misinterpreted, not only by the public, but also by artists themselves. One of the most common errors in this respect arises in the fact that the intuitive—or better, the unconscious—attitude of an artist is often confused with his deliberate intellectual attitude towards reality and life. In many great writers these two attitudes are antagonistic, and if the intellectual attitude gets the upper hand, the artist may gradually merge into the ' thinker ' and moralist. Unfortunately, in such cases, the public seeks and finds his significance chiefly in the moralising and ideological froth of his creation, forgetting that this may have little or nothing to do with the intrinsic value of his art.

Such a misunderstanding happened, for instance, with Tolstoy. Thanks only to the critical insight of Dmitry Merezhkovsky, we begin at last to realise that the unconscious message of Tolstoy as artist, is more important, more profound and original than his philosophical and moralistic effusions. We can even see that Tolstoy the artist was at his best in complete contradiction with the one-sided ascetic Tolstoy of the *Kreutzer-Sonata* and the rationalistic-religious pamphlets.

Something of the kind also occurred with regard to another modern spirit, Henrik Ibsen, whose deliberate ideas and watchwords have been too often taken as the kernel of his work. Did not the feminists claim the great Norwegian as the representative and even the apostle of their 'idea'? And so did the anarchist-individualists, the moralists, and *tutti quanti*—oblivious of the fact that such an attitude may conceal rather than reveal the true Ibsen.

II

In the case of Ibsen, indeed, the mistake is more than natural, for there is hardly another great modern writer who has so impregnated his art with deliberate 'Ideas.' At the first glance he seems to be the most ideological artist of our time. And yet the ideas, as such, were neither the aim nor the end, but only the material, the means, of his writings. Instead of dissolving his art in his ideas, he dissolved his ideas in his art. Instead of going through reality to ideas, he tried to penetrate through contemporary ideas to the very core, to the naked truth, of

contemporary reality. Being himself one of
those sensitive personalities in whom are focussed
all the main spiritual values and strivings of our
time, he tested their real relation to the Individual
and to Life. The problem of individualism,
the woman question, the sexual problem, the
problem of evolution—all found in Ibsen not
their propagandist, but their judge and vivisector.

'To create is to hold a severe trial of one's
self,' is one of his sayings, which may be completely applied to his own works. Like all true
creators, he was constantly pushed forward to
new questions and problems, by an inner—one
might say, by an ethical—need to discover his
own significance, his own self-realisation in the
realm of deceitful actualities. His spirit wandered
in the chaotic labyrinth of contemporary ideas
and values as in a vast cemetery—amidst the
haunting ghosts and shadows. 'I almost think
we are all of us ghosts,' says his Mrs Alving.
'It is not only what we have inherited from our
father and mother that "walks" in us. It is
all sorts of dead ideas, and lifeless old beliefs,
and so forth. They have no vitality, but they
cling to us all the same, and we cannot shake
them off. Whenever I take up a newspaper, I
see ghosts gliding between the lines. There
must be ghosts all the country over, as thick

as the sands of the sea. And then we are, one and all, so pitifully afraid of the light.'

It was this horror of 'ghosts' that compelled Ibsen to look for a way out of the cemetery of our actual life, a way towards the awakening, the 'resurrection' of the dead. But while he sought as a hopeful idealist and optimistic 'philosopher,' his innate scepticism was always busy dissecting, analysing, and paralysing.

III

This double process is one of the most characteristic features of Ibsen's art, a feature which may easily be observed in the majority of his greater plays, especially in those of the second half of his literary activity. Taken as a whole, Ibsen's writing was mainly conditioned by these two antagonistic tendencies, although by his incredible skill he generally succeeded in welding them into more or less unitary works of art. This antagonism may even give, as we shall see, the key to the peculiar technique of Ibsen's drama.

As the themes are usually conceived by Ibsen the 'philosopher'—by a mere intellectual process, as it were—his plays often seem deliberate and intentional; his characters also appear, on the whole, to be put into the general scheme with the precision of a mathematician. But while his rather scientific intellect provides the skeleton, his artistic intuition builds up the body of the work. As soon as the whole intentional scheme is complete, there begins a subtle working of the artist and psychologist. The skeleton may be shaped according to the dictates of one or another 'Idea,' yet this rarely involves the subjugation of Ibsen's subsequent intuition to any preconceived purpose and tendency: it only gives to it the direction, and this once fixed, the 'intuitive' process strives to develop towards its own independent conclusions.

And so it happens that the unbiassed artist and psychological observer in Ibsen gradually undermine his own ideology with all its *pia desideria*, and even convert Ibsen, the resolute idealist, into the tragic pessimist, capable of ironising and destroying in his later dramas what he had exalted in the earlier ones.

How pathetic he is, for instance, in *Brand*, with his uncompromising battle-call:—

' Now but in shreds and scraps is dealt
  The Spirit we have faintly felt;
  But from these scraps and from these shreds,

These headless hands and handless heads,
These torso-stumps of soul and thought,
A Man complete and whole shall grow,
And God His glorious child shall know,
His heir, the Adam that He wrought.'

And, like a Titan, he asserts:—

' Mine is that Will and that strong Trust,'
That crumbles mountains into dust !

Compare this ' strong Trust' with the doubtful and wavering Rosmer, with the bankrupt
Borkman, and especially with the sculptor Rubek,
who also started his vocation as an idealist—
with the vision of the Resurrection Day,
embodying it in the figure of a ' young unsullied
woman awakening to light and glory.'
' But I learned wisdom in the years that
followed, Irene,' he acknowledges at the end.
' The " Resurrection Day " became in my eyes
something more, and something—something
more complex. The little round plinth on which
your figure stood erect and solitary—it no longer
afforded room for all the imagery I now wanted
to add. . . . I imagined that which I saw with
my eyes around me in the world. I had to include
it—I could not help it, Irene. I expanded the

plinth—made it wide and spacious. And on it I placed a segment of the curving, bursting earth. And up from the fissures of the soil there now swarm men and women with dimly-suggested animal faces. Women and men as I knew them in real life. . . .'

The whole line from *Brand* through *Peer Gynt*, *Ghosts*, and especially *The Wild Duck*, to the cold and cruel *John Gabriel Borkman* and *When We Dead Awaken*, is but the result of this paralysing wisdom of Rubek. The closer Ibsen looked at the enigma of man and life the more haunted he was by it; and whenever he tried to find a safe refuge in ' positive ' ideas or ideals, his inner honesty compelled him to undermine, sooner or later, his own refuge. He is not a convinced idealist, but only a Tantalus of ideals.

True, if we examine some of his plays singly, we may easily prove that Ibsen tried to affirm, or even propagate, some ' ideal,' but as soon as we take his creation as a whole and find the inner bond between his works, such a view will appear not only one-sided, but even misleading. For however passionately Ibsen wished to build, he was always compelled—against his own will—to be a destroyer. Not building, but destroying was his true element, or, at least, his destiny.

IV

Besides, if we examine Ibsen's so-called ideals and constructive ideas separately from his art, we see that as ' prophet ' and builder he has not much to say. As has been often observed, his diagnosis of the great Invalid, called Modern Society, is always penetrating; but his prescriptions are neither original nor daring. Most of them are at present even out of date. Apart from this, they seem as cold as his entire attitude towards Reality and Life, which on the whole is not religious (in the sense of an all-embracing Sympathy), as in the greatest artists of mankind, but rather 'rationalistic.' He blames and condemns not out of love, but out of indignation. Behind his works we feel too much a stern and brooding sociologist, or a severe physician; and, as a rule, we are impressed more by the greatness of his will than by the greatness of his soul. His very inner pathos is not the pathos of a passionate soul, but the pathos of a passionate will. However, it is not the passion that leads him to the ideas, but rather the ideas that lead him to the passion. And the more rebellious and protesting the idea, the stronger is the creative emotion kindled by it.

Ibsen and his Creation

That is why Ibsen instinctively clings to protest and revolution from the very beginning of his literary activity. It was the stormy year of 1848 that gave him the first creative impulse (his youthful play *Catilina* was written in 1848, in the name of protest), and protest was the *leitmotiv* of most of his later works.

He is, in fact, one of the sturdiest 'protestants' in modern European literature. As such, he always knew what to deny, but he never was quite sure what to affirm, for in the course of time, his 'self-anatomy' stripped one ideal after the other to their bare skeletons. And preferring to be untrue to the ideals rather than to himself, Ibsen gradually arrived at those lonely 'heights' where his soul began to freeze in the thin and icy atmosphere of its own 'spiritual emancipation.' Instead of the great Resurrection Day, he found at the end of his journey emptiness and the cold silence of the desert.

He wrapped himself in this silence, looking as enigmatically on his admirers as Rubek must have looked on those who extolled the artistic execution of his busts, without suspecting beneath them the hidden, revengeful thought of the creator who paid for his art with the happiness of his own life.

12

Ibsen's Dramas and the Drama of Ibsen

'There is something equivocal, something cryptic, lurking in and behind these busts—a secret something that the people themselves cannot see. . . . I alone can see it. And it amuses me unspeakably. On the surface I give them the " striking likeness," as they call it, and they all stand in astonishment—but at the bottom they are all respectable, pompous horse-faces, and self-opinionated donkey-muzzles, and lop-eared, low-browed dog-skulls, and fatted swine-snouts, and sometimes dull, brutal bull-fronts as well. . . .'

This is how Rubek characterises his own sculptures, and these words may well be true of the ' double-faced ' plays of Ibsen, also. In almost every one of them there is a ' secret something that the people cannot see.' But penetrating from their outward masks to this 'something' is the same as penetrating through Ibsen's dramas to his personal Drama—to that inner working of which his plays were but sporadic symbolical flashes.

CHAPTER II
IBSEN AS ARTIST

II

I

BROADLY speaking, we can distinguish among artists those who are satisfied with being only litterateurs and artists, and those who try to rise *through art* beyond the sphere of mere art. The former usually sacrifice the Man to the Artist, being often great in art but small in life; the latter look upon the creation of great art as a step towards the creation of great life, rating the perfect Man higher than the perfect Artist.

Such an attitude may, however, lead to an interesting mental conflict—the conflict between Man and Artist. This conflict is often encountered among the Northern writers, especially among the Russians. The inner tragedy of Gogol, for instance, was his inability to find a synthesis between the creation of art and the creation of life; he fell at last into a vague mysticism in which he burned the completed manuscript of the second part of his best work,

Dead Souls. The Polish poet, Adam Mickiewicz, also became a religious mystic, and so did Julius Slowacki, the Polish Shelley. A particularly striking example in modern times, however, is Tolstoy, who, in his old age, condemned almost cynically his earlier works of ' pure ' art, and became the active preacher of a new life.

Ibsen also is one of those who look upon the creation of art as a means to the creation of Life. He hated mere æstheticism with its dogmatic *l'art pour l'art*, considering it as dangerous to true art as dogmatic theology is to true religion. At the same time, he combined his intellectualised ethical impulses with his art so skilfully that generally he avoided the danger to which even so great an artist as Tolstoy succumbed.

This danger is the ' tendency,' the moral ' purpose,' which is always lurking at the cross-roads where the ethical and the æsthetic directions meet. Most of Ibsen's works were originated just at this meeting place, and yet he subdued his creative material to his artistic tact in such a remarkable way as to reconcile factors which were apparently irreconcilable.

Some glimpses into the inner process of Ibsen's method may give us, in a certain degree, the explanation of this interesting phenomenon.

Ibsen as Artist

II

It has already been stated that Ibsen usually began his works as 'philosopher' and carried them out as artist. This is sufficiently demonstrated by the first drafts of some of his plays. Among the preliminary notes for the famous *Doll's House* we find, for instance, the following remarks :—

'There are two kinds of spiritual law, two kinds of conscience one in man and another, altogether different, in woman. They do not understand each other; but in practical life the woman is judged by man's law, as though she were not a woman but a man. . . .

'Woman cannot be herself in the society of the present day, which is an exclusively masculine society, with the laws framed by men and with a judicial system that judges feminine conduct from a masculine point of view. . . .

'A mother in modern society is like certain insects who go away and die when they have done their duty in the propagation of the race.'

Among the first notes for *Ghosts* we read :—

'Marriage for external reasons, even when

these are religious or moral, brings a Nemesis upon the offspring. . . .

'These women of the present day, ill-used as daughters, as sisters, as wives, not educated according to their gifts, prevented from following their inclination, deprived of their inheritance, embittered in temper—it is these who furnish the mothers of the new generation. What is the result ? . . .

'The key-note is to be : The prolific growth of our intellectual life, in literature, art, etc.— and in contrast to this: the whole of mankind gone astray. . . .

'Among us monuments are erected to the dead, since we have a duty towards them; we allow lepers to marry, but their offspring——? The unborn—— ? '

And again, among the rough drafts of the *Lady from the Sea*, we find:—

'Has the line of human development gone astray ? Why have we come to belong to the dry land ? Why not to the air ? Why not to the sea ? The longing to possess wings. The strange dreams that one can fly and that one does fly without being surprised at it—how is all this to be interpreted ? . . .

' Human beings akin to the sea. Bound by the sea. Dependent on the sea. Compelled to return to it. A fish species forms a primitive link in the chain of evolution. Are rudiments thereof still present in the human mind ? In the minds of certain individuals ? . . .

' The sea possesses a power over one's moods that has the effect of a will. The sea can hypnotise. Nature in general can do so. The great mystery is the dependence of the human will on that which is " will-less." '

III

It is evident that these notes could have been much more easily extended into sociological and psychological essays than into plays. And yet, instead of dry dissertations on feminine mentality, etc., Ibsen created the charming Nora (perhaps the most living and womanly character in contemporary drama), Mrs Alving, Oswald, Ellida Wangel, and a whole gallery of other figures. His plays, as a whole, are as far from being dramatised treatises as they are from being dramatised ' tendency.'

The solution of this riddle is simple : instead of illustrating and preaching his ideas through drama, Ibsen individualised them, incarnated them in living characters. He went from ideas to reality, not in order to violate or distort reality by applying ready-made formulæ to it, but to make the ideas *live* in a new and transmuted reality. This proceeding is exactly opposite to that of the 'tendency-writers.' Instead of giving us plays with a ' moral ' imposed upon them, he embodies in them their own organic philosophy.

Ibsen himself was quite conscious of this attitude towards 'moral' and moralising. In a letter to Brandes (1871) concerning *Emperor and Galilean*, he acknowledges that his new play would be a ' sort of banner,' but he adds immediately:—

' Do not be afraid, however, of any tendency-nonsense. I look at the characters, at the conflicting designs, at history, and do not concern myself with the moral of it at all. Of course, you will not confound the moral of history with its philosophy; for that must inevitably shine forth as the final verdict on the conflicting and conquering forces.'

And many years later when the Norwegian Women's Rights League arranged (in 1898) a festival at which the author of the *Doll's House* was hailed as a preacher of feminism, Ibsen replied somewhat brusquely:—

Ibsen as Artist

'I am not a member of the Women's Rights League. Whatever I have written has been without any conscious thought of making propaganda. I have been more poet and less social philosopher than people generally seem inclined to believe. I thank you for the toast, but must disclaim the honour of having consciously worked for the Women's Rights movement. I am not quite clear as to just what the Women's Rights movement really is. To me it has seemed a problem of humanity in general. And if you read my books carefully you will understand this. True enough, it is desirable to solve the problem of Women's Rights, along with the others; but that has not been the whole purpose. My task has been the *description of humanity.*'

How slow, thorough, and methodical was this ' task ' we may gather from the fact that Ibsen devoted to the elaboration of each of his later plays about two years, during which time he filled his ' philosophy ' drop by drop with blood and life, weighing and reckoning every sentence, every word, every movement and pause with admirable psychological tact and technical skill, thus giving us often a curious resultant of calculation and intuition, one might almost say, a resultant of artifice and art.

Ibsen and his Creation

Ibsen is not rich in variety of characters. From his first dramatic attempt down to *John Gabriel Borkman* we encounter, again and again, variations of the two types of women represented by Furia and Aurelia in *Catalina*, and by Hiordis and Dagny in *Vikings at Helgeland*— Ibsen's first masterpiece. Nor are his single characters rich in colour; expressive and intense, they may rather be said to be carved out of stone than painted. They usually complete each other on the principle of *chiaroscuro*, all the details being arranged in such a way as to form a compact dramatic whole, and to point out through their very realism the symbolical *arrière-pensée* of the author, avoiding all that is purely accidental. There is, in fact, nothing superfluous either in the characters, in the scenery, or in the architecture of Ibsen's plays. Every trifle is worked out with the utmost precision, almost with pedantry.

This mathematical strictness induced the talented Scandinavian writer, Knut Hamsun, to refer rather contemptuously to Ibsen (in his book *Mysterier*) as a dramatic ' book-keeper.' However, it is often due to this very book-keeping that Ibsen achieves that dynamic intensity of development and structure, which is so characteristic of his plays.

24

In the first half of his literary activity, Ibsen was considerably under the influence of the French drama of mere plot and situations. But as soon as he came to regard the intrigue, as well as the characters, *sub specie* of some ' idea ' or other, he was led gradually by corresponding changes in technique, to the so-called Ibsenian play. Intrigue for the sake of intrigue lost its former importance for him, and in transferring the centre of gravity to the ' philosophy ' and psychology of the characters he naturally emphasised the inner at the expense of the external drama. The consequence was that the external dramatic action and movement were reduced to a minimum, to be replaced by the inner dramatic tension. With this object Ibsen (in his later works) put the tragic guilt of his heroes into the past, *i.e.* outside the acted drama. By partial confessions, by mysterious hints and allusions to previous guilt, he creates from the very beginning of the play that peculiar ' Ibsenian ' atmosphere which draws our attention so strongly to the inner working of the characters. The external catastrophe itself is for Ibsen only a pretext and symbol of an inner transformation.

Brand, Bernick, Nora, Rita Allmers, Solness, Rubek—they all emphasise in and through their catastrophe that new 'truth' which caused in them a radical inner change.

Ibsen's skill in this respect is so great that by the very poverty of external dramatic action he usually makes the drama still more dynamic, saturating it with the inner content. He knows how to achieve the maximum of effect by the minimum of means. Where a Victor Hugo would pour out floods of rhetoric, Ibsen limits himself to a few laconic words and pauses. By his structure he succeeds in concentrating in simple, unpathetic expressions the highest dramatic pathos. And it is just here that Ibsen's dramatic 'book-keeping' and artistic tact go hand in hand, to produce a dynamic, a 'condensed' reality whose essence may also elucidate for us Ibsen's symbolism.

v

To realise this symbolism it would first be necessary to draw a definite line between organic and inorganic symbols, or rather between Symbol and Allegory. Since this subject is extensive as it is interesting, we shall try to point out at least the most important differences.

While allegory illustrates an 'idea,' symbol incarnates it organically. Every allegory is an abstraction of the reality, while the symbol is a new reality in itself and by itself. Allegory is therefore static and 'intellectual,' symbol dynamic and emotional. The former we ' understand,' the latter we comprehend with our whole being. Allegory often narrows our conception of reality, symbol enlarges and deepens it. Moreover, a truly symbolic work may be differently accepted and experienced by every individual in every age—without the slightest loss of its inner power. In the course of centuries each generation finds in it a new creative content and inspiration. The *Prometheus Bound* was felt quite otherwise by the ancient Greeks than it is by us; none the less it remains for us an equally great work of art. And so only a symbolic work is permanent, for its intrinsic force is not paralysed by the changing and growing values of humanity, but is transmuted by them, without losing its vitality.

If we apply the above characteristics to the works of Ibsen, we see that Ibsen's symbolic strength lies not in his deliberate ' symbols,' but in his condensed and dynamic realism. In the individual tragedies of many of his characters, we feel concentrated the tragedy of the whole

27

of contemporary society. Ibsen illuminates the petty events of the provincial Norwegian circles in such a way as to give them a universal significance. He deepens the drama of local society until it becomes the drama of Humanity. And the more realistic he is in such cases the greater is the symbolical significance of his realism.

On the other hand, when Ibsen endeavours to operate with deliberate symbolism, he is nearer to allegory than to symbol. Sometimes he balances between them, paying alternate tribute to both; and when he escapes inorganic allegorism he does so only by using his ' symbols ' as auxiliary means to his condensed realism; in other words, by trying to absorb the symbols in the characters and not *vice versa*.

Thus Ibsen's symbolism may be defined simply as a transmutation and deepening of reality; and this transmutation is always dictated by some individual questioning, seeking and striving.

Therefore, in spite of his reforms in contemporary drama, Ibsen always gives the impression of being far more interested in new forms of life than in new forms of art. ' Everything that I have written has the closest possible connection with what I have lived through, even if it has not been my own personal—or actual—

experience,' he writes in a letter to L. Passarge; ' In every poem or play I have aimed at my own spiritual emancipation and purification—for a man shares the responsibility and the guilt of the society to which he belongs.'

And in one of his optimistic moments, which became so rare towards the end of his life, he tried to formulate, amongst others, his view of art and life in his Stockholm speech (1887) as follows: ' It has been said that I, and that in a prominent manner, have contributed to create a new era in these countries. I, on the contrary, believe that the time in which we now live might with quite as good reason be characterised as a conclusion, and that from it something new is about to be born. For I believe that the teaching of natural science about evolution has validity also as regards the mental factors of life. . . . I believe that poetry, philosophy, and religion will be merged in a new category and become a new vital force, of which we who live now have no clear conception.

As far as Ibsen's art is concerned, he actually endeavoured to make of it such a ' new vital force.' For this reason his literary work is a continuous attempt to blend Philosophy with Art and Art with Life. And in this attempt he persevered to the end.

CHAPTER III
The Strength of his Weakness

III

THE STRENGTH OF HIS WEAKNESS

I

It is a commonplace that the main-spring of contemporary artistic creation is not strength, but weakness posing as strength. Our ' creative ' stimuli are of a negative kind: beneath them lies, as a rule, mere protest, mere vindictive reaction against life and reality. Being inwardly too empty to create out of the surplus of his own vitality, the modern artist seeks all the more insistently for strong external means by which to kindle his creative impulses and prove his strength—not so much to others perhaps, as to himself.

The usual means adopted in such cases is the protest or rebellion which arises in the ' will to power' and becomes more a 'psychological' than an ethical necessity: one simply wants an external enemy on whom to test and prove one's strength in order to believe in it. Revolt against society, against the age or against mankind, may give one more than sufficient of that inner tension which is so often mistaken for strength; and the more intense the rebellion, with its aggressive criticism, the stronger the feeling, or rather the illusion, of power. Other plausible illusions may be provided by the noisy egotistic 'individualism' and the so-called spiritual aristocratism with its 'pathos of distance,' its fussy inner pride and scorn.

It would lead us too far to investigate the 'decadence,'—all the different aspects and disguises of the creative poverty of contemporary art and literature. The posing egotism, the so-called romanticism, the iconoclastic futurism, the emasculated æstheticism, and the many other 'isms' bear witness that we cry for strength only in order to forget how weak, doubtful, and bankrupt we are. A penetrating psychology of our modern 'protestants,' professional rebels, and deliberate pessimists (*i.e.* passive rebels), would discover many surprising, not to say unpleasant things. The most interesting point, however, is that these eternally criticising, eternally rebelling spirits would become still more unhappy if a sudden fulfilment of their aims took place. They probably would then react against perfection in the same manner as they are now reacting against imperfection; they would rebel against their own former rebellion. For their secret is not that they want perfection, but that they want protest as such, and therefore a permanent pretext for it, since this is the only disguise for their sterility and almost the only remaining stimulus to creation.

It is symptomatic that even Nietzsche, one of the subtlest spirits of our age, is in many respects an illustration of what has just been said. His very cry for the ' will to power ' is a proof of his lack of power. And on close examination of Ibsen's works and personality we come to the conclusion that Ibsen himself, this manly and virile artist, belonged in part to the same category.

1736157

II

During the whole of his first period Ibsen was tortured by doubt of his creative ' power,' of his poetical vocation. His early plays even give the impression that he wrote them chiefly in order to prove to himself that his true meaning and destiny was to be a ' skald.' Great protest, great heroic figures of Viking-times, great sorrow, great indignation—everything that could strengthen his wavering creative impulse, was welcomed. As early as in 1858 he wrote to his friend, Carl Anker: 'Believe me, it is not agreeable to see the world from the October standpoint; and yet there was, strange to say, a time when I wished for nothing better. I had a burning desire, I almost prayed, for a great sorrow which might round out my existence and give life meaning.'

And yet his doubts often seemed stronger than himself. How great and oppressive this self-mistrust was, we may gather from the colossal figure of Jarl Skule (in *Pretenders*).

'Tell me, Jatgeir, how came you to be a skald? Who taught you skaldcraft?' asks the doubting King Skule of the bard Jatgeir.

'Skaldcraft cannot be taught, my lord.'

'Cannot be taught? How came it, then?'

'The gift of sorrow came to me and I was a skald.'

'Then 'tis the gift of sorrow the skald has need of?'

'I needed sorrow; others there may be who need faith or joy—or doubt——'

'Doubt as well?'

'Ay; but then must the doubter be strong and sound.'

36

' And whom call you the unsound doubter ? '

' He who doubts his own doubt.'

' That, methinks, were death.'

' 'Tis worse, 'tis neither day nor night! '

And the brooding Jarl Skule adds here ' quickly, as if shaking off his thoughts ':—

' Where are my weapons ? I will fight and act—not think.'

Something of this kind is often to be found in a modern doubter of himself who deliberately seeks for struggle—in order to paralyse his doubts. And the stronger his ' will to power ' the more he yearns for external enemies with whom to fight. In order to justify his protest and strengthen his impetus, he may even require an ethical sanction, which eventually can lead to the self-delusion that he has been sent by a higher Power, by God Himself, to do great things—as a reformer, teacher, judge, or ' prophet.' He struggles against the whole ' compact majority,' and the consciousness of being alone only emphasises the illusion of his power. He endeavours to drown his doubt in passionate criticism of all and everything, and, particularly in a fanatical insistence upon his individual ' mission.' Considering his subjective *idée fixe* as the only truth, and all that does not agree with it as falsehood and error, he accepts (with a strange inner pleasure) injustice, anger, even martyrdom, as long as they appear to justify his standpoint and invigorate the power of his protest.

It was in the period of his greatest doubtfulness that the unacknowledged poet Ibsen declared through Falk (in *Love's Comedy*, 1862):—

'. . . the battle flag I'll rear!
Yes, it is war I mean with nail and tooth
Against the Lie with the tenacious root,
The lie that you have fostered into fruit,
For all its strutting in the guise of truth.'

And a few years later (1867) he writes to Björnson, concerning the bad reception of *Peer Gynt* by the public: ' However, I am glad of the injustice that has been done to me. There has been something of the God-sent, of the providential dispensation in it; for I feel that this anger is invigorating all my powers. . . . If it is to be war then let it be war! If I am no poet, than I have nothing to lose. I shall try my luck as photographer. My contemporaries in the North I shall take in hand one after the other. I will not spare the child in the mother's womb, nor the thought or feeling that lies under the word of any living soul that deserves the honour of my notice. . . .'

The Strength of his Weakness

Or take the significant passage from Ibsen's letter to Peter Hansen (1870): 'During the time I was writing *Brand* I had on my desk a glass with a scorpion in it. From time to time the little animal was ill. Then I used to give it a piece of soft fruit, upon which it fell furiously and emptied its poison into it—after which it was well again. Does not something of the same kind happen with us poets? The laws of nature regulate the spiritual world also.'

But while struggling fiercely with all the 'liars that are dupes of their own lie,' he occasionally makes private confessions of great interest. Among his complaints to Brandes that Rome had been taken away from human beings and given to the politicians, he exclaims, in 1870: 'Where shall we take refuge now? All that is delightful—the unconsciousness, the dirt—will now disappear; for every statesman that makes his appearance there, an artist will be ruined. And then the glorious aspiration after liberty— that is at an end now. Yes—I must confess that the only thing I love about liberty is the struggle for it; I care nothing for the possession of it.'

In another letter we read: 'He who possesses liberty otherwise than as a thing to be striven for, possesses it dead and soulless. . . . So

that a man who stops in the midst of a struggle
and says: " Now I have it "—thereby shows
that he has lost it. It is, however, exactly this
dead maintenance of a certain given standpoint
of liberty that is characteristic of the communities
which go by the name of states—and this is
what I called worthless.'

And again: 'Dear friend, the Liberals are
freedom's worst enemies. Freedom of thought
and spirit thrive best under absolutism; this was
shown in France, afterwards in Germany, and
now in Russia.'

In short, it is not liberty and truth, but rather
the struggle for them that matters. The struggle
for principles and ideals is perhaps more important than ideals themselves—-which, by the way,
are not absolute and permanent. For ' neither
the conceptions of morality nor those of art are
eternal. To how much are we really obliged to
pin our faith ? Who will vouch for it that two
and two do not make five up in Jupiter ? ' And
in another passage, ' All development hitherto
has been nothing more than a stumbling from one
error into another. But the struggle is good,
wholesome, and invigorating.' It was this
struggle which inspired many themes of his plays
—the struggle of the individual against Society,
State, tradition, Church, against the ' ghosts '

and the sick consciousness of the whole age, and finally even against his own struggle.

Hence Ibsen may even give the impression of consciously preferring the dark side of life to ' heaven's light,' perhaps suspecting that the latter might paralyse his impetus and indignation. He is like his ' Miner ' who wanders in the ' mountain's living womb,' and finding there nothing but a growing darkness, asks:—

> ' Have I failed, then ? Does the way
> Lead not to the upper day ?
> Yet I know the heaven's light
> Would but blind my dazzled sight.'

And therefore goes on striking for striking's sake:—

> ' What though darkness be my lot,
> Strike my hammer, falter not;
> What though every hope be vain.
> Strike my hammer, strike again.'

III

Closely connected with this attitude is Ibsen's individualism of the ' alone-standing,' whose tendencies are, however, less innocent than one might at first suppose. For it easily may involve a practical application of his advice to Brandes (in 1871): 'What I chiefly desire for you is a genuine, full-blooded egoism, which shall force you for a time to regard what concerns you yourself as the only thir_g of any consequence and everything else as non-existent.'

One step further, and we reach that obsession with one's subjective points of view which end in various kinds of ego—mania. Ibsen himself is a typical 'alone-stander,' and as such he is conspicuously devoid of that generous expansiveness and radiation which are the signs of rich natures. There is often even something mean and grudging about his 'individualism' which ostracises *a priori* any kind of solidarity. 'I have never really had any firm belief in solidarity,' he confesses; 'in fact, I have only accepted it as a kind of traditional dogma. If one had the courage to throw it overboard altogether, it is possible that one would be rid of the ballast which weighs down one's personality most heavily.'

On another occasion he wrote to Brandes: 'I hear you have organised a society. Whether you may be strengthening your position or not, I cannot tell; to me it appears that the man who

stands alone is the strongest. . . .' And object-
ing to his having translated Mill's *Utilitarianism*,
he acknowledged: ' I must honestly confess that
I cannot in the least conceive of any advancement
or any future in the Stuart Mill direction.
I cannot understand your taking the trouble to
translate this work, the sagelike philistinism of
which suggests Cicero and Seneca.'

In emphasising the ' duty towards one's self '
against the duty towards the collective, he went
so far as to shun friends and friendship, for they
are ' an expensive luxury; and when a man's
capital is invested in a calling and a mission in
life, he cannot afford to keep them. The costli-
ness of keeping friends does not lie in what one
does for them, but in what one, out of considera-
tion for them, refrains from doing. . . .'

Thus he proclaims, ' Be thyself fully,' and, at
the same time, he shuts his own Self from the
collective life like a miser, lest his individuality
should wither. Or as he says in one of his
letters: ' There are actually moments when the
whole history of the world appears to me like
one great shipwreck, and the only important
thing is to save one's self.'

And yet, in spite of his somewhat spinster-
like self-assertiveness, Ibsen was not superficial
enough to regard this kind of salvation as the

highest aim of one's striving, still less one's true self-realisation. What is more, the end of *Brand*, and many pages in *Peer Gynt*, prove that he profoundly suspected the real psychological basis of such an egotistic individualism. Already in *Brand* and *Emperor and Galilean* he made a desperate endeavour to overcome it and to find ' anything tenable in the present situation —with its untenable ideals.' He tried to find that positive and over-individual aim which should bring his personal will into harmony with a higher will and value. But in this search he came up against an impassable barrier.

In order to understand what this barrier was we must analyse Brand, Peer Gynt, and Julian the Apostate; for, in spite of all their outward differences, there exists a profound inner connection between these three figures.

CHAPTER IV
THE DRAMA OF THE MORAL SUPER-MAN

IV

THE DRAMA OF THE MORAL SUPERMAN
(*The Dilemma of Brand*)

I

IT is not difficult to discern in modern humanity a more or less achieved differentiation between the religious and the moral consciousness. Owing to various more or less complicated reasons, moral values have, so to speak, cut themselves off from religious values, aiming at an independent existence.

This tendency, however, has proved dangerous not only to religion, but also to morals. For the more autonomous and emancipated morality becomes, the more it loses its over-individual basis and *raison d'être*. Robbed of the latter, our moral instinct naturally arrives either at a purely utilitarian justification which leads towards compulsory civic ' virtues ' and mechanical moral drill, or at moral self-will and anarchy. A third peril lies in narrow puritanism, which tends towards moral pride, with its- self-complacent

47

and very unethical consciousness of personal ethical perfection. This frequently occurs in Protestantism, which made, by the way, one of the most notable attempts to subdue the religious to the moral consciousness. But the more the former is engulfed by the latter the more moralising does religion become, until it degenerates into a mere dry and formal code of moral duties.

True, in many modern individuals the moral consciousness is already beginning to realise the ultimate consequences of its complete autonomy; and in order to avoid them it is instinctively seeking again a firmer basis and a higher impersonal justification—in religious consciousness. But just when religious consciousness is most needed and desired, we find that it is almost atrophied.

Being aware of this deficiency, we try, none the less, to become religious ' on principle.' Failing a true religious consciousness we strive at least for its intellectual substitute—a religious *Weltanschauung*, and this again we usually form according to our moral ' principles.' Instead of going from religion to morals we move from ready-made morals to ready-made religion, often mistaking moral recipes for religion itself. But the stronger the will which operates in this way, the

48

more complete may be the misunderstanding, not only of Religion, but also of Life. The highest assertion of the personal will may lead in such a case to one-sidedness and even to the violation of life, in spite of our good intentions: for moral impulses—if dictated only by moral principles—usually turn out to be the fiercest tyrants, opposing all the joy of life, denying and condemning everything that does not submit to them. A strong moral will, severed from a profound religious consciousness and religious love, is the origin of a fanatical moral intolerance which is the more narrow and dangerous the more genuine the impulse in which it arises—especially when the moralist sees in it a higher ' mission.'

It is one of our great misfortunes that, seeing the insufficiency of the irreligious attitude towards life, we have a *will to Religion*, and yet are incapable of the religious will—that will which alone can reconcile the sternest moral exigencies and duties with the greatest fullness and joy of life, thus asserting life in its totality. Hence the growing cleavage of our will between its hedonistic and its moral impulses. So complete has this cleavage become that the tendency towards a full self-assertion in either of these directions leads to a dead-wall against which the individuality is invariably shattered, unless it finds a synthetic

49

outlet on the plane of religious consciousness.

Many illustrations of this could be found in
everyday life, in contemporary art and thought.
Among modern spirits Henrik Ibsen may be
pointed out as a typical instance of the highly
developed moral consciousness, allied to a feeble,
almost non-existent religious consciousness.

This fact gives the clue not only to his personal
seeking and inner drama, but also to all his main
characters. And nowhere is his personal tragedy
better revealed than in *Brand*. This powerful
dramatic poem is the ripest work of the first half
of Ibsen's literary activity, and is at the same
time a profound attempt at spiritual self-portraying
and self-anatomy. ' Brand is myself in my best
moments,' confesses Ibsen; and indeed, Brand's
dilemma helps us to understand many of the
motives of Ibsen's later plays, and also Ibsen
himself.

II

First of all, we discover in Brand a typical
moralist endowed with a tremendous will which
endeavours to assert itself, according to his moral
principles.

The Drama of the Moral Super-Man

' It is Will alone that matters,
    Will alone that mars or makes,
Will that no distraction scatters,
    And that no resistance breaks.'

That is his motto. And with this will ' that
no resistance breaks ' he declares war on all that
is ' human too human,' war on average man, on
average virtue, on average sin, on all that is
' light-heart, faint-heart, and wild-heart,' thus
protesting against his whole sick age. He sees
his mission in nothing less than the re-fashioning
of man and earth.

' It is our age whose pining flesh
    Craves burial at these hands of mine.'

And, in so far as he blames and whips all the
spiritual pettiness, shallowness, and cowardice of
his age, he is great and magnificent. With his
unswerving, uncompromising ' all or nothing '
he stands among his weak and will-less fellow-
creatures as a Titan among pygmies. The only
thing he sees before him is his individual ' call,'
the great moral mission he has to fulfil. But
the more he is absorbed by this task, the more
narrow and cruel becomes his will to everything
that does not fully coincide with it.

Already in Brand's first meeting with Einar
we see Ibsen's main antithesis: the antithesis
between the hedonistic and the moral conception of life—between the joy of life and its
' call.'

> ' In sunshine lies our destined way,
> And ends but with a hundred years.
> A hundred years to revel given,
> Each night the bridal lamp aflame—
> A century of glorious game. . . .'

Thus exults the merry bridegroom Einar,
thinking of the joy of life and not caring
very much for its deeper ' call.' But the
stern Brand with whom he is confronted
answers:—

> ' Ye will but laugh and love and play,
> A little doctrine take on trust,
> And all the bitter burden thrust
> On One who came, you have been told,
> And from your shoulders took away
> Your great transgressions manifold.
> He bore for you the cross, the lance—
> Ye therefore have full leave to dance;
> Dance then,—but where your dancing ends
> Is quite another thing, my friends.'

The Drama of the Moral Super-Man

It is this 'quite another thing, my friends' with which Brand is concerned. He appears in the very beginning of the drama as the greatest hero of the 'Categorical Imperative' in modern literature; and as such he is ready to sacrifice for its sake not only his own happiness, but that of everybody else.

And this is what he actually does. Wishing 'completely to fulfil' only his moral self, he resolutely opposes it to all 'earthly' things—to joy, to happiness, to passion. Instead of a full and harmonious self-realisation, the puritan super-man Brand asserts only one part of his total self—by ascetic renunciation, by repressing all instincts and impulses which impede him in his spiritual self-conquest and moralised 'will to power.' He is strong in his renunciation and heroic struggle, but his will is destructive and in essence irreligious, in spite of all its morality. Brand's Ego does not transcend and widen itself in a mystical religious fusion with God. On the contrary, he narrows God to the size of his own moral imperative. His God is nothing but the projection of his moral megalomania, and at the same time a protesting dialectical antithesis to the compromising 'God' of Einar and his kind:—

' Ye need, such feebleness to brook,
  A God who'll through his fingers look,
  Who, like yourselves, is hoary grown,
  And keeps a cap for his bald crown.
  Mine is another kind of God! . . .'

And here Brand describes Him in the same
manner as he would describe and symbolise his
own puritanical Will to Power. His God
turns out to be—

'. . . young like Hercules,
  No hoary sipper of life's lees!
  His voice rang through the dazzled night
  When He, within the burning wood,
  By Moses upon Horeb's height
  As by a pygmy's pygmy stood.
  In Gideon's vale He stay'd the sun,
  And wonders without end has done,
  And wonders without end would do,
  Were not the age grown sick—like you.'

III

Thus, the God of Brand is not *Deus caritatis*,
but *Deus voluntatis*—a fiction of Brand's own will
to moral self-assertion for the sake of which he

sacrifices all his happiness, the salvation of his
mother, the lives of his son and wife, and finally
even his own life. In his titanic but narrow
striving he is as cruel and pitiless towards himself
as towards others. His tremendous will has
laid, as it were, icy fetters upon his soul—in
order to arrive at a full triumph. Therefore,
love, human love, is foreign to him; more, it is
his greatest danger, for it may weaken the impetus
of his ' call.' To him ' the sovereign Love is
Hate,' and it is hatred that emphasises his protest
and his moral indignation. Conforming not
his will to God (whom he does not know), but
his god to his will, he arrives at a supreme moral
Egotism and unconscious moral pride. Brand
becomes a saint and even a martyr—out of moral
pride. His wife, Agnes, divines one of his
profoundest features when she exclaims:—

' How stern! It is thy pride of will
   That scorns the darkness and the chill! '

Therefore, the more ' moral ' his will becomes
the less religious it is, and in the difference
between these two wills lies also the difference
between Brand and Christ. Brand's Christianity
is as far from Christ as that official Christianity
against which he struggled.

IV

Brand tries to subdue Life to his ' call ' in order to assert his individual puritan will. And the results we see first in Agnes, grieving on Christmas Eve for her dead child—sacrificed to Brand's ' pride of will.'

> ' Closed, all closed with bolt and bar!
> Seals on every passion set! '
> Seal'd the grave and seal'd the sky,
> Seal'd to feel and to forget!
> I will out!   I gasp for breath
> In this lonely house of death.'

We see them again, on a big scale, in the last act, where the flock follows Brand like a new Messiah in expectation of the great miracle which should renew earth and life. However, it is not great Will alone that performs miracles. At the critical moment the moralist Brand has nothing to offer his followers—nothing but his Will, and renunciation for the sake of the Will. Therefore he is deserted and stoned by the people, who go back to their valley, seduced by the compromising and cunning 'vultures of the law.'

The persecuted and lonely Brand takes refuge

among the icy peaks of the mountains, far from men and the world, in the company of the mad Gerd. And here begins the subconscious reaction against his ' Categorical Imperative.'

It would lead us too far to analyse the tremendous nightmare phantoms, doubts, and new temptations which there haunted Brand's weary and disillusioned spirit. Everything which he was longing for crumbled away, even the faith in the power and efficiency of his superhuman Will.

> ' Worm, thou may'st not win His spirit—
> For Death's cup thou hast consumed;
>   Fear his will, or do not fear it,
>   Equally Thy work is doom'd.'

Thus sings the Invisible Choir in the sough of the storm. Tortured by hopelessness, by despair, by the wild images of his own madness, Brand at last exclaims—as though cursing his heroic struggle, for whose sake he has banned all the sunlight, happiness, and joy of life :—

> ' Hence! a thousand miles away!—
> How I long to fly afar,
>   Where the sunlight and the balm
>   And the holy hush of calm,
>   And Life's summer-kingdoms are!'

Here, in his terrible defeat, he begins to realise that the God of Will is not yet the God of Life. Bursting into helpless tears, he guesses that Christ is far from him, since he does not know His great Love.

> ' Jesus, I have cried and pleaded—
> From Thy bosom still outcast;
> Thou hast pass'd me by unheeded
> As a well-worn word is passed,
> Of salvation's vesture, stain'd,
> Let me clasp one fold at last.'

And, in his humiliation—after his ' pride of will ' has vanished—Brand attains what he could not attain in his proud struggle; weeping, ' radiant, and with an air of renewed youth,' he perceives a new light.

> Through the Law an ice-track led—
> Then broke summer overhead!
> Till to-day I strove alone
> To be God's pure tablet-stone;
> From to-day my life shall stream
> Lambent glowing, as a dream.
> The ice-fetters break away,
> I can weep—and kneel—and pray! '

Something new, something which has been fettered hitherto by his cruel puritanism, now flares up. He is on the verge of Religion, but here comes the retribution. The thunder of an avalanche grows louder and louder; and crouching under the descending snowy mass, Brand exclaims in death-anguish:—

> 'God, I plunge into death's night,
> Shall they wholly miss Thy light
> Who unto man's utmost might
> Will'd—— ?'

The avalanche buries him, and through the thunder a Voice answers: 'He is—God of Love!' (Han er—*Deus caritatis!*) . . .

Thus Ibsen himself undermined, perhaps contrary to his own intention, the loveless puritan Brand, whose striving Will was moral, but not religious. One could even add that a Will which is only 'moral' is for this very reason immoral.

CHAPTER V
THE 'PEER GYNT' SELF

V

THE 'PEER GYNT' SELF

I

AFTER having launched the drama of the heroic moralist Brand, Ibsen examined—with equal artistic power—the reverse side of the same problem. This he undertook in *Peer Gynt*, which may be looked upon as one of his most serious works, in spite of all its polemical and even journalistic passages.

The chief character in this dramatic poem is the opposite of Brand. While Brand represents a great tragedy of Personality, Peer Gynt embodies its tragi-comedy. Brand attempts to subdue the whole of life to his moralised individual will and, therefore, through his very moral greatness, he commits an outrage upon Life; Peer Gynt, on the other hand, subdues his will to life, and so commits an outrage upon himself. Brand sacrifices his happiness to his ' call '; Peer Gynt prefers to sacrifice all his inner ' calls ' to the joys and pleasures of life. While Brand's will is

63

centripetal, the will of Peer Gynt is centrifugal,
or, rather, it is without any centre at all. Instead
of the straight line of Brand's unbending will,
we find in Peer Gynt the ' curved line ' of eternal
compromise—compromise with himself, with
reality, with God, and the Devil. Brand's categorical, ' Be thyself! ' undergoes at the hands
of Peer a complete transvaluation in the name
of his notorious ' Gyntish Self.'

> ' The Gyntish Self—it is the host
> Of wishes, appetites, desires—
> The Gyntish Self, it is the sea
> Of fancies, exigencies, claims,
> All that, in short, makes my breast heave,
> And whereby I, as I exist. . . .'

That is Peer Gynt's philosophy of the Self.
He substitutes for individualism its antithesis—
egoism. As a typical egoist, he naturally becomes
a slave of his own appetites and fancies, disguis-
ing them under individualistic labels. Brand's
striving ' All or nothing ' degenerates in Peer
Gynt into ' all and nothing ' with its formula:
' Be self-sufficient! ' That is why Peer equally
easily becomes a troll, a merchant, a slave-trader,
a Bible-trader, a financier, a ' scientist,' a ' prophet'
and so on. He can turn into anything for the

very reason that he has strangled his real Self. He is all, and, at the same time, nothing. Or, as his father-in-law, the old troll of Dovre, characterises him,—

'So willingly, in short, did we find him in all
    things,
I thought to myself the old Adam, for certain,
Had for good and all been kicked out of
    doors.'

Always true to his ' Gyntish Self,' he travels from one appetite to another, from one selfish fancy to another, justifying each by his own conception of the principle, ' Be thyself.' After his adventure with Anitra—for whose sake he lost not only his high rank as a ' prophet ' but also his money and treasures—he met at the pyramids of Giseh the learned Doctor Begriffenfeldt. This man listened with admiration to Peer's conception of individualism, and in order to introduce him to a number of others initiated in the same cult, invited him to his residence —the madhouse of Cairo. And there the great moment takes place: no sooner does Peer enter the hall than he is recognised by all the madmen as their natural chief. They greet him as their king, while Doctor Begriffenfeldt

exalts their own 'Gyntish Selves' in ecstatic
rapture,—

> ' We go, full sail, as our very selves,
>   Each one shuts himself up in the barrel of
>   self,
>   In the self-fermentation he dives to the
>   bottom—
>   With the self-bung he seals it hermetically,
>   And seasons the staves in the well of self,
>   No one has tears for the other's woes;
>   No one has mind for the other's ideas.
>   We're our very selves, both in thought and
>   tone,
>   Ourselves to the spring-board's uttermost
>   verge.'

Surrounded by the raving madmen, Peer Gynt
faints and sinks down on the floor. In the
meantime, they crown him as the great ' Emperor
of Himself '—

> ' Ha! see him in the mire enthroned,
>   Beside himself—to crown him now!
>   Long live, long live the Self-hood's Kaiser!
>   *Es lebe hoch der grosse Peer!* '

The ' Peer Gynt ' Self

II

After this apotheosis of the ' Gyntish Self ' we meet Peer Gynt as an old and gray-haired man, sailing back to his native country. The ship on which he is travelling is suddenly wrecked, and the worthy Peer sends the cook of the ship to the bottom in order to save himself, little troubled by the fact that the man's numerous children at home are doomed thereby to starve.

Finally, we see him again in the haunts of his youth, and here an inner reaction commences. Remembering his young days and adventures, Peer Gynt begins to perceive his whole life in its true aspect. A terrible doubt gnaws his soul, and for the first time he seems to divine the truth of his ' Gyntish Self.' He begins to realise that his life has been without any meaning, and his personality without any kernel—like the onion he picked up and peeled on the way: ' To the innermost centre is nothing but swathing—each smaller and smaller. Nature is witty! '

Pondering over his past, he dimly guesses that he has lost his Self—through his selfishness; that ' self-realisation ' in the name of the Gyntish Self has been nothing but a slow destruction of

67

all his inner possibilities, faculties, and ' calls.'
And while he is looking in astonishment upon
the ruins of his true personality, strange voices
begin to pursue him: his unthought thoughts,
his unproclaimed ideas, unsung songs, unshed
tears, unachieved deeds—all demand an account
from Peer Gynt. In anguish he tries not to
listen to them; he wants to escape, but they
beset and haunt him everywhere like ghosts. At
a crossways he is stopped at last by the Devil
himself (the Button Moulder), who claims his
Soul in order to melt it down and destroy it
for ever as worthless rubbish.

Peer protests against such a punishment.
During his whole life he has served only his
dear self, and how can he now consent to its
absolute annihilation! To such an unpleasant
prospect he would prefer all the torments, all
the eternal pains of hell. He therefore defends
himself; he wants to prove that in his sins he
was not worse than other people:—

' I'm sure I deserve better treatment than this;
I'm not nearly so bad as you think—
Indeed, I've done more or less good in the
world;
At worst you may call me a sort of a bungler,
But certainly not an exceptional sinner.'

This argument, however, fails of its due effect, for the Button-Moulder gives a quite unexpected answer:—

' Why, that is precisely the rub, my man!
  You're no sinner at all in the higher sense;
  That's why you're excused all the torture-
      pangs,
  And, like others, land in the casting-ladle! '

In other words, Peer's greatest sin is that he has not realised himself either through virtue or through sin. He belongs to those of whom it is said : ' So, then, because thou art lukewarm, and neither cold nor hot, I will spue thee out of my mouth.' His Soul is doomed to be ' spued out,' to disappear for ever in the ' waste-box.'

For a while he manages to escape on a pretext; but at the next crossways the implacable Button-Moulder pops up again. And now there is only one way of salvation for Peer—to prove that he really is himself. If he cannot do that, he is lost. He endeavours to find a single proof, but the obstinate logic of the Button-Moulder is stronger than Peer's proofs.

' One question—just one,' he exclaims at last in despair. ' What is at bottom, this being oneself ? '

And here he learns the secret of true self-realisation.

'To be oneself is: to slay oneself' (*i.e.* to slay one's Gyntish Self), answers the Button-moulder, and adds:—

'But on you that answer is doubtless lost,
And therefore we'll say: to stand everywhere
With *Master's intention* displayed like a sign-
    board.'

Peer Gynt asks:—

'But suppose a man never has come to know
What Master meant with him?'

The Button-Moulder:—

'He must *divine* it. . . .'

'But how often are divinings beside the mark
—then one is carried *ad undas* in middle career,'
remarks the puzzled Peer Gynt, and the Button-
Moulder cuts him short with a not very com-
forting reply:—

'That is certain, Peer Gynt; in default of
    divining
The cloven-hoofed gentleman finds his best
    hook.'

70

After such a reply there remains to Peer nothing but the exclamation:—

' This matter is excessively complicated. . . .'

III

On a closer examination the matter indeed proves to be ' excessively complicated '—not only to Peer Gynt, but also to Ibsen, who in these passages touches upon the profoundest riddle of individual self-assertion. For, in more sober language the argument of the Button-Moulder can be reduced to this: true individual self-realisation is possible only in the name of an over-individual Will and Value, while self-assertion in one's own name leads towards self-destruction.

Without going into further details, Ibsen allows Peer to capitulate and acknowledge with resignation that in this higher sense he never was himself:—

' I no longer plead being myself;
  It might not be easy to get it proven,
  That part of my case I must look at as
      lost. . . .'

In regret and sorrow he prepares to leave the Earth whose grass he had trampled ' to no avail.'

> ' I will clamber up high, to the dizziest peak;
> I will look once more on the rising sun,
> Gaze till I'm tired o'er the promised land;
> Then try to get snowdrifts piled over me,
> They can write above them: Here no One
>   lies buried. . . .
> I fear I was dead long before I died.'

That is Peer's sentence upon himself, upon his ' Gyntish Self.'   At the last moment, however, a miracle occurs: Peer's soul is saved from the ' waste-box ' by the beloved of his young days in whose heart he has been preserved ' as the whole man, the true man.'

> ' Where was I, as myself, as the whole man,
>   the true man ?
> Where was I, with God's sigil upon my
>   brow ? '—

he exclaims on the threshold of Solveig's hut, and Solveig, who has been waiting for him, her whole life long, answers:—

> ' In my faith, in my hope, and my love. . . .'

Solveig's pure love paralyses the power of the Button-Moulder; none the less, Peer's life is forfeited. It has been sacrificed to the ' Gyntish Self.'

IV

In *Brand* Ibsen proclaimed that ' it is Will alone that matters '; but, in the same drama, he demonstrated clearly enough that Will alone is not sufficient. In *Peer Gynt* he developed this theme further until he came to the conclusion that a true self-realisation can be achieved only in harmony with our ' Master's intention,' which we have, however, to divine; for unless we divine and accept it, our Individualism is doomed to degenerate into its very antithesis, into Egoism and Egotism.

But here the question arises, How are we to divine our ' Master's intention ' ? How are we to bring our Will into harmony with His Will ? In other words, how can we arrive at a religious self-assertion, especially if we are not religious ? And whose guilt is it that we are not, that we cannot be, religious—in spite of our passionate longing to be so ?

It is here that Peer Gynt's dilemma becomes

our own dilemma, and his tragedy ours. For even suppose that we seriously try to divine our 'Master's intention,' where is the guarantee that we have really divined it ? Was not the moralist Brand fanatically persuaded of having divined it ? And yet, at the end, the 'Master' Himself told him (in the manner of a modern *deus ex machina*) that he was wrong !

But if we cannot 'divine' it, what are we to do with our Will ? Moreover, who is in such a case responsible for our mistake—we or the 'Master' ?

Ibsen tackled this problem of the Will in his next drama, *Emperor and Galilean*.

CHAPTER VI
The Tragedy of the Will

VI

THE TRAGEDY OF THE WILL

I

IBSEN'S ' world-historic ' drama, *Emperor and Galilean*, is justly classed among his less successful works from the artistic standpoint. Apart from the fact that it is one of his most studied productions, we feel that its architecture is far from being satisfactory. Its figures, too, are schematic and bloodless; even its chief character, the Emperor Julian, is psychologically badly sustained, for often we are uncertain (especially in the second part) whether we have before us a real tragic hero of the Will, or a caricature of such a hero. On the whole, the play might easily give us the impression of having been written not by a great dramatist, but by an able professor of dramaturgy.

And yet, it is characteristic of Ibsen that he himself obstinately regarded this very play as his ' chief work '—a peculiarity which can be explained only on the assumption that through this drama he tried to express himself much more fully than is at first apparent. Some proofs to this effect we find, in truth, in his letters of that period. 'I am putting,' he wrote in 1872, 'into this work a part of my own spiritual life; what I depict, I have, under other forms, myself gone through, and the historic theme I have chosen has also a much closer relation to the movement of our own time than one might at first suppose.' And in another letter he states that 'there is in the character of Julian more of my own spiritual experience than I care to acknowledge to the public.'

From Ibsen's further utterances on this subject we gather that in some respects it really was so, particularly in the ideological respect —and we have seen already how great an importance Ibsen attached to 'ideas' in his works. But we know also that his creation was the result of the simultaneous and antagonistic processes of a striving ideologist and of a burrowing sceptic. Sometimes the former is contradicted by the latter in a subsequent work; sometimes during the elaboration of the same play, and that quite openly as, for instance, in *Brand*; sometimes, again, Ibsen masks the divergence, and we must dive beneath the surface in order to find out the hidden discord. *Emperor and Galilean* is a typical instance of such a duality. This is confirmed not only by the analysis of the drama itself, but also by Ibsen's private confessions. Thus, in a letter of July 12, 1871, he writes to his publisher, Hegel: 'I am hard at work on *Emperor Julian*. This book will be my chief work, and it is engrossing all my thoughts and all my time. That positive theory of life which the critics have demanded of me so long, they will get in it.' However, in spite of this optimistic promise, he writes to Brandes a few weeks later (September 24) in a strikingly different tone and mood: 'And so I ought to raise a banner, ought I? Alas, dear friend! That would be much the same kind of performance as Louis Napoleon's landing at Boulogne with an eagle on his head. Later, when the hour of his destiny struck, he needed no eagle. In the course of my occupation with Julian, I have in a way become a fatalist.'

To this duality of mood corresponds also the duality of the drama itself. Ibsen genuinely tries in it to put forward a 'positive theory of life,' and surreptitiously he himself cuts the ground from under it.

II

The basic problem of *Emperor and Galilean* is again, as in *Brand* and *Peer Gynt*, the problem of the Will. But Ibsen here attempted to go further than in those two plays, and therefore his 'philosophical,' as well as psychological, conclusions are of great interest. We saw in *Brand* Ibsen's antithesis of the joy and the 'call' of life. Brand's will is directed exclusively toward the stern moral call which kills all joy and happiness. In Emperor Julian, however, the will takes the opposite direction—towards the great and sunny joy of life. The two antitheses struggle here for a final victory, one of them being represented by the Christian God of renunciation, and the other by the laughing gods of Olympus.

This rather schematic contrast is, of course, neither new nor original; but it is just through its interpretation and generalisation that Ibsen endeavours to express his 'positive' message. Like Dostoevsky, he sees in the struggle between 'flesh and spirit' not a commonplace theological dilemma, but the profoundest dualism of man's consciousness—that permanent split in our Will which leads eventually to the split in our ethical impulses and values. 'My play,' writes Ibsen,

' deals with a struggle between two irreconcilable powers in the life of the world—a struggle which will always repeat itself. Because of this universality, I call the book a world-historic drama.'

This struggle, in fact, has never perhaps been more tragic than in our epoch. We are at last aware that renunciation for the sake of the spirit makes the spirit itself sick and lame; at the same time we feel that the assertion of our ' flesh ' against the spirit leads towards the destructive ' Gyntish Self.' Wavering between them we are unable to suppress either the one or the other, and yet we cannot find a reconciliation and synthesis. We may rebel against our moral imperatives with their categorical ' Thou shalt '; we may reject them by our intellect, by our ' healthy soul,' but when we try to crush them, it is ourselves who are crushed by them. We are in their power—in spite of our logic, in spite of our rebellion.

' Always " Thou shalt." If my soul gathered itself in one gnawing and consuming hate towards the murderer of my kin, what said the commandment: " Love thine enemy." If my mind, athirst for beauty, longed for scenes and rites from the bygone world of Greece, Christianity swooped down on me with its " Seek one thing

needful." If I felt the sweet lusts of the flesh
towards this or that, the Prince of Renunciation
terrified me with his " Kill the body that the
soul may live." All that is human has become
unlawful since the day when the seer of Galilee
became ruler of the world. Through Him, life
has become death. Love and hatred, both are
sins. Has He, then, transformed man's flesh
and blood ? Has not the earth-bound remained
what he ever was? Our inmost, healthy soul
rebels against it all—and yet we are to will in
the very teeth of our own will ! Thou shalt,
shalt, shalt ! '

Thus laments the Emperor Julian, in whom
Ibsen believed he had found an appropriate
illustration of our own inner division as well.
The old sensual beauty of the naïve and innocent
' beyond good and evil ' has been destroyed by
the Christian impulse which awakened and
carried to the utmost limits our moral consciousness. Hence the new Truth came into collision
with the old Beauty, the one becoming a negation
of the other.

In order to evade the resulting cleavage, Julian
deliberately directs his will towards the old
Beauty, unaware of the fact that man's consciousness, once having been pregnant with the
new Truth, can never again still its voice, and

that after Christ we cannot return to Olympus:
we must either go forward to a higher synthesis,
or perish under the burden of our own duality.
Besides, in his struggle against the new Truth
for the old Beauty, Julian himself begins to appre-
hend that ' the old beauty is no longer beautiful,
and the new truth is no longer true. . . .'

But here appears the mystic Maximus with
his vision of a new state of human consciousness.
He sees the possibility of overcoming our inner
split not in the return to the innocent Homeric
amorality, but in a new supermoral beauty which
will reconcile flesh and spirit, Apollo and Christ.
The fierce duel between the Emperor Julian
and the Galilean cannot, therefore, finish in the
suppression of the Galilean by the Emperor,
or vice versa. And so when Julian asks, which
of them shall conquer, Maximus answers:—

' Both the Emperor and the Galilean shall
succumb. . . . I say you shall both succumb—
but not that you shall perish. Does not the
child succumb in the youth, and the youth in
the man ? Yet neither child nor youth perishes.
. . . The empire of the flesh is swallowed up in
the empire of the spirit. But the empire of the
spirit is not final, any more than the youth is.
You have striven to hinder the growth of the
youth—to hinder him from becoming a man.

Oh, fool, who have drawn your sword against that which is to be—against the third empire, in which the twin-natured shall reign ! . . . Emperor-God—God-Emperor. Emperor in the kingdom of the spirit—and God in that of the flesh. . . .'

So Julian strove, not for the third, but for the first empire. And he perished.

III

This is more or less the ' philosophical' skeleton of the drama. But though Ibsen does his best to promulgate 'that positive theory of life which the critics have demanded so long,' we still can trace the working of the hidden vivisector, who arrives at somewhat less ' positive' conclusions.

While the 'philosopher' in Ibsen endeavours to find an aim which will fully reconcile and assert our striving Will, the vivisector tries to penetrate, through ' self-anatomy,' into the ultimate mystery of the Will itself. Realising that we can assert our Self through our Will only in so far as the Will is really free, Ibsen naturally wanted to investigate the limits of its freedom. In these excursions, however, he did not escape the fate of other explorers of the Will: like them he became entangled in various logical and psychological contradictions. One of these puzzling contradictions, discovered by Julian, is the fact that we will—even against our own Will. Or, as Julian exclaims: ' Our inmost healthy soul rebels against it all; and yet we are to will in the very teeth of our own will! Thou shalt, shalt, shalt! . . .'

Once conscious of that, we involuntarily arrive at the hackneyed question : if we do this, is not our will then under the spell of necessity, our relative freedom being merely apparent ? Peer Gynt did not assert himself because he did not divine his ' Master's ' Will. But how could he, if our Will is nothing but a blind tool of the ' Master,' or perhaps of a mysterious World-Will which repeats its ' circles of the eternal return ' with the dull and indifferent regularity of a terrible machine ? In such a case is not even our freedom of choice only illusory ? For we will what we must will; we are the dupes and victims of a pre-destined cruel Necessity. Individual self-assertion with its ' Be thyself fully,' moral responsibility, personal mission, the ' call ' and the meaning of life—all these are then nothing but illusion and self-delusion. That is why the mystic Maximus

85

exclaims, when terrified by this supposition:
'What is it worth to live? All is sport and
mockery. To will is to have to will. . . .'

But a strongly ethical character like that of
Ibsen cannot endure such a supposition. Putting
the meaning of life higher than life itself, he is
bound to destroy life as soon as the meaning of
life has been destroyed. Therefore, even where
he is logically compelled to assume the law of
Necessity, he inquires how far we are free in
Necessity itself. If there is a universal over-
individual Will, what is its relation to our
personal will? Where does our freedom cease,
and where begins the law of Necessity?

But in spite of our efforts, there is no
definite answer to this question—at least, within
the limits of our earthly mind. We may return
to the problem of freedom again and again, but
as soon as we try to solve it, we stumble, like
Ibsen in *Emperor and Galilean*, over a new riddle.
Take, for instance, the scene of the symposium
in Ephesus, during which Maximus evokes
spirits.

'What is my mission?' asks Julian, of the
first of the conjured spirits.

'To establish the Empire—by the way of
freedom,' answers the Voice.

'Speak clearly! What is the way of freedom?'

' The way of necessity.'

' And by what power ? '

' By willing.'

' What shall I will ? '

' What thou must.'

Maximus then conjures up the spirit of Cain.
On the question of his own individual ' call '
in life, Cain answers that his mission has been
his sin; and that he has sinned because he has
been himself.

' And what didst thou will, being thyself ? '

' What I must. . . .'

' And what fruit has thy sin borne ? '

' The most glorious. Life.'

' And the ground of life ? '

' Death.'

' And of death ? '

' Ah, that is the riddle. . . .'

After Cain, Maximus talks to the spirit of
Judas, and Julian is eager to know what has
been Judas's individual mission in life:—

' The twelfth wheel of the world-chariot,'
answers Judas.

' Whither did it roll by means of thee ? '

' Into the glory of glories.'

' Why didst thou help ? '

' Because I willed.'

' What didst thou will ? '

' What I must.'
' Who chose thee ? '
' The Master.'
' Did the Master foreknow when he chose
thee ? '
' Ah, that is the riddle. . . .'

IV

Thus, while inquiring after the limits of our
' freedom in necessity,' we risk arriving at the
conclusion that the ' Master ' Himself may be
under the law of Necessity, or rather identical
with an irresponsible, *i.e.*, blind and unconscious,
World-Will, whose works are ' sport and
mockery.' But as long as there is no incontestable solution of this dilemma, there is no
incontestable direction for our moral consciousness either: all our values of good and evil are
then relative and uncertain.

From the problem of ' freedom in necessity,'
we so come to the problem of Absolute Value,
which, by the way, was the main ' psychological '
problem of Dostoevsky's novels. Dostoevsky
passionately forced himself to find an escape
from his cul-de-sac on that religious plane where
necessity and freedom ought to coincide (in so

far as we realise our active inner union with the
' Master '); Ibsen, on the other hand, remained
coldly halting between his philosophic vision
of the Third Empire and the fatalistic
absolutism of the ' world-will.'

' The world-will has laid an ambush for me,
Maximus,' exclaims Julian, while dying of a
wound, in Phrygia. And over his body Maximus
laments: ' Wast thou not, then, this time either
the chosen one—thou victim on the altar of
necessity ? . . . What is it worth to live ?
All is sport and mockery. To will is to have to
will. . . .'

But the ' prophet' in Ibsen did not quite
capitulate; for, what would then have become
of his promised ' positive theory of life ? ' No
sooner did Maximus utter his desperate cry
than he corrected himself: ' But the Third Empire
shall come! The spirit of man shall re-enter
its heritage.'

And in this vision Ibsen endeavoured to
believe, in spite of the fact that he had become
'in a way a fatalist' during his occupation with
Julian. Even much later—in his Stockholm
speech in 1887—he emphasised again the vision
of Maximus. Apparently it was not so easy to
give up the only ' positive theory of life ' he
could discover.

CHAPTER VII
THE DUEL WITH THE 'GHOSTS'

VII

THE DUEL WITH THE 'GHOSTS'

I

IN *Brand*, *Peer Gynt*, and *Emperor and Galilean*, Ibsen reached his greatest spiritual tension. In his excursions into the eternal problems of life he stopped, however, on the line which divides a philosophic from a religious mind. Both his method and his mentality prevented him from entering the consciousness of the 'Third Empire.' In his intense search for a creative value of life he encountered, besides, too many inner contradictions; it was natural, therefore, that after *Emperor and Galilean* he should temporarily descend from his dizzy heights to modern social problems in their various aspects and replace 'self-anatomy' by the anatomy of society.

On this plane he found much material for his protestant and warlike temper. Criticising and unmasking all the conventional social lies and ideals, he fought now not for new spiritual

93

values, but first of all for a complete emancipation
from inherited and worn-out values; he strove
for that inner liberty which alone can make us
ripe for a new life. ' Is it only in the domain
of politics that the work of emancipation is to
be permitted to go on with us? Must not
men's minds be emancipated first of all?
Men with such slave-souls as ours cannot
even make use of liberties they already
possess.'

Proclaiming the sovereignty of the Individual
as against the herd, he logically protested against
all the ties, laws, and institutions imposed upon
the Individual by the community in order to
'enslave' him. Already in 1870 he wrote in a
letter : ' Undermine the idea of the State; make
willingness and spiritual kinship the only essen-
tials in the case of a union—and you have the
beginning of a liberty that is of some value.
The changing of forms of government is mere
toying with degrees—a little more or a little
less—folly the whole of it.' And in 1882 he
stated again: ' I have not the gifts that go to
make a satisfactory citizen, nor yet the gift of
orthodoxy; and what I possess no gift for, I
keep out of. Liberty is the first and highest
condition for me. At home they do not trouble
very much about liberty, but about liberties—a

few more or a few less, according to the standpoint of their party.'

This ethical and aristocratic anarchism gave
strength to his blows in proportion to the
tension and distance between him and the society
whose pitiless judge he now became. With the
objective coldness of a scientist he examined,
judged, and condemned all the social ' ghosts '
and life-lies. But in dealing blows at one life-
lie after another, he soon reached (in *Wild Duck*)
that region where life and falsehood are so
organically interwoven that the destruction of
falsehood would imply the destruction of life
itself. With a melancholy resignation, Ibsen
then took, apparently at least, the side of life
and changed once more his themes, and also his
militant mood.

II

Leaving aside the vivid, but not particularly
important *League of Youth* (published before
Emperor and Galilean), we come to *Pillars of
Society*, which opens the social plays with truly
Ibsenian satire and sarcasm. Here, as in many
of his other plays, Ibsen projects movements,
problems, and ideas of the ' great world ' into

the small and petty society of Norwegian Philistines, and in this projection all their inherent defects naturally become more salient. None the less, the sarcasm of the *Pillars of Society* is, in spite of its virulence, good-humoured rather than gloomy and pessimistic. Ibsen shows simultaneously Bernick's vileness and his inner regeneration, as well as his own belief in such a regeneration. Ceasing to be a respectable ' pillar,' Bernick reconquers his better self with the help of Lona, who proclaims at the end that ' the spirits of Truth and Freedom are the true pillars of society.' Thus the ' positive' principles triumph after all.

The attack delivered in this play was more stinging than bold. Equally stinging but much more subtle and daring was the next—the famous *Doll's House*, in which Ibsen produced the highest dramatic tension simply by the skilful antithesis between a cosy bourgeois idyll and the impending tragedy. This tension rapidly increases until the inevitable explosion takes place—with a moral lesson from Nora, it is true; but as her lesson has a sufficient psychological motivation, the play scarcely suffers from it: it remains a *chef-d'œuvre* in spite of the moral.

The more deeply Ibsen penetrates into the problems of contemporary social life, the more

stern and gloomy he becomes, as witness *Ghosts*
—that masterpiece of what one may call symbolic
realism. In the *Doll's House* Nora repudiates
her duty towards her husband and children for
the sake of her duty towards herself; nevertheless, in the finale of the play there is almost
a promise of that ' miracle of miracles ' which
would convert the communion between man and
wife into a real marriage. In *Ghosts*, however,
we find no belief in miracles. ' The fault lies
in that all mankind has failed,' Ibsen writes in
his preliminary notes for this play, in which he
so resolutely strips the naked life-truth of all
official ' ideals.' We hear how Pastor Manders,
the professional guard of such ideals, admonishes
the mother of Oswald, Mrs Alving :—
' Is there no voice in your mother's heart that
forbids you to destroy your son's ideals ? '
' But what about the truth ? '
' But what about ideals ? '
' Oh! Ideals! Ideals! If only I weren't such
a coward! '
The whole drama is permeated with a dark
despair, with fog and rain. And the cry of the
mad Oswald for the sun makes the atmosphere
only more hopeless, more ghastly.
After this violent attack upon ' ideals ' Ibsen
attempted to give them a new blow in his *Enemy*

of the People, but, this time, the result was somewhat disappointing: the play is relatively weak,
chiefly because of Ibsen's too obvious desire
that it should be strong. A great deal of its
dynamics is, in fact, dissolved in didactic rhetoric.
The worthy Dr Stockman, who discovered
(among his other ' discoveries ') that ' all our
sources of spiritual life are poisoned, and that
our whole society rests upon a pestilential basis
of falsehood,' makes too much noise when
declaring war on the ' compact majority '—with
the vocabulary of a thundering leader-writer in
a radical provincial newspaper. He produces
a somewhat comic impression for the very reason
that he is supposed to be as sincere in his pathos
as once Brand was in his. It is hardly worth
while to enunciate with such heroic gestures a
' discovery ' like this: ' In a house that isn't
aired and swept every day—my wife, Katrine,
maintains that the floors ought to be scrubbed
too, but we can't discuss that now;—well—in
such a house, I say, within two or three years,
people lose the power of acting morally. Lack
of oxygen enervates the conscience.'

With all his militant individualism (' the
strongest man is he who stands alone ') Stockman
has not the mentality of a spiritual aristocrat,
but that of a spiritual parvenu; there is too much

self-admiration in his honesty and truthfulness. This moral self-complacency reminds one almost of a 'righteous' sectarian. Moreover, the difference between Ibsen's former tragic fighters (Brand and Julian), and the well-intentioned Dr Stockman is not only in their intensity, but also in their inner convincingness. 'All who live upon lies should be exterminated like vermin!' exclaims Stockman, and at the same time he himself acknowledges that 'a normally constituted truth lives, as a rule, seventeen or eighteen years; at the outside twenty; seldom longer. . . .'

Are, then, such truths worth fighting for? But the matter is evidently not so much in the truths as in the fighting itself. Indeed, Ibsen seems to have made Stockman so loud and rhetorical that he might lull himself and calm the re-awakening sceptic, who was gradually beginning to react against the idealist. This new reaction soon burst forth in its full strength in *The Wild Duck*.

III

In this remarkable play we find the conclusions at which, as it were by the back door, the sceptical and vivisecting double of Ibsen arrived—despite

all his moralising and 'positive' intentions.
Ibsen gave in it a condensed picture of life in
its vulgar everyday aspect, which is all the more
hopeless for the very reason that it is not even
aware of its own hopelessness. The characters
had acclimatised themselves to the marshy atmosphere of lies to such an extent that lies became
life itself. Destroy the lies of these people, and
you destroy their lives.

Ibsen raised his hand for the sake of the
truth, but now he began to waver in delivering
his blow. Is it worth striving, if mankind has
hopelessly failed, and if lies are as necessary
to people as crutches to a lame man ? Dr
Stockman wanted to exterminate like vermin
all those who live upon lies; the philosophy of
The Wild Duck, however, suddenly turns out to
be the opposite. In Hialmar's declamations one
discerns even a deliberate parody of Ibsen's
former ethical claims and formulæ about duty
towards oneself, etc. 'There are certain claims
—what shall I call them ?—let me say claims
of the ideal—certain obligations, which a man
cannot set aside without injury to his soul,'
repeats Hialmar Ekdal like a parrot—in order
to do with an easy conscience just the contrary.

Or take the pitiful role of Gregers Werle
with his 'mission'! This sentimental moralist

is a bloodless shadow, or, better, an involuntary
caricature of Brand. While Brand wanted to
regenerate the whole of mankind, Gregers
humbly sees his 'call' in establishing a new
life among the hopeless Philistines, Hialmar,
and his wife Gina—'a communion founded
on truth and free from falsehood of any
kind.' This 'mission' issues tragi-comically
for Hialmar and Gina, but with catastrophe for
the little Hedvig and for Gregers himself. And
after all, the philosophic or ideological verdict is
this time expressed not by the ' positive ' Gregers,
but by his cynical antipodes, Dr Relling, who
preaches life-lies as the only means to go on living,
and even deliberately inoculates with them the
great ' inventor ' to be, Hialmar, as well as the
wretched drunkard, Molvik, whom he makes
' dæmonic.'

' That is the blister I have to put on his
neck.'

' Isn't he really dæmonic, then ? ' naïvely asks
Gregers.

' What the devil do you mean by dæmonic ?
It is only a piece of hocus-pocus I've invented to
keep him alive. But for that, the poor harmless
creature would have succumbed to self-contempt
and despair many a long year ago.'

And here he passes the following sentence

upon Gregers and his claims: 'Oh, life would be quite tolerable after all, if only we could be rid of the confounded duns that keep on pestering us, in our poverty, with the claim of the ideal.'

'In that case I am glad that my destiny is what it is,' answers Gregers.

'Excuse me—what is your destiny?'

'To be the thirteenth at the table. . . .'

Such is the finale of this work, about which Ibsen himself wrote in 1884 to F. Hegel, when sending him the manuscript: 'In some ways this new play occupies a position by itself among my dramatic works; in its method it differs in several respects from my former ones. But I shall say no more on this subject at present.'

It is regrettable that he actually said 'no more on this subject.' However, one can guess that in *The Wild Duck* the 'positive' Ibsen came again to a blind alley, as it were, and once more undermined himself. After such a work, the virulent struggle with life-lies must needs lose a great deal of its inner impetus and even sincerity. The creative energy must either find a new outlet or degenerate into a moralising rhetoric, on the dangerous verge of which Ibsen had already arrived in his *Enemy of the People*. But he so admirably balanced the two antagonistic elements of his creative process that, whenever he felt a danger from the watching vivisector, he always passed in time to new motives and problems. Thus, after the philosophic *Emperor and Galilean* he went over to social plays, and after *The Wild Duck* to 'psychological' dramas. In these he resumed the analysis of the individual consciousness and examined from a fresh point of view the dilemma which he had already treated in *Brand* and *Emperor and Galilean.*

CHAPTER VIII
The 'Sickly Conscience'

VIII

THE 'SICKLY CONSCIENCE'

I

IBSEN's psychological plays begin with *Rosmersholm*, in which the social and political background is merely a canvas for the inner drama of Johannes Rosmer and Rebecca West. Here we see Ibsen cautiously returning to the great problem of Brand and Julian—this time not on a romantic or metaphysical plane, but on the plane of our everyday life and moral experience. The dilemmas are now decreased in magnitude and for this very reason nearer to us; the heroes are no more moral supermen like Brand, but characters of the same flesh and blood as ourselves; they are everyday men in heroic and tragic perspective.

We saw how Brand sacrificed all his happiness in life to the ' call ' of life with its ' Categorical Imperatives '; how Julian strove for the opposite values, and how at last the ' call ' itself became an uncertain metaphysical problem, wholly depending on the solution of the insoluble riddle of the Will. And Ibsen could not bridge over this split and reconcile in a higher religious synthesis the two poles represented by Brand and Julian, since his mentality was only moral without being religious.

A solely moral consciousness is even bound to widen the cleavage and to lead towards a further disintegration of personality and life—in so far as its imperatives lay a ban on joy and earthly happiness. Our will remains split between the 'call' of life and the joy of life, permanently wavering between them, and unable to affirm either the one or the other. But as soon as the value of the 'call' proves to be insoluble or risks becoming a self-delusion, a deliberate reaction against it may take place: the impulse towards happiness and joy grows stronger —until it dashes itself anew against the moral consciousness, against the 'sickly conscience.'

'If one had a really vigorous, radiantly healthy conscience—so that one *dared* to do what one *would!*'

But one does not dare, for together with our inner development grows our 'sickly conscience' —in spite of all logic and reason. The most important problem that arises from such a position is, of course, the question whether our conscience is a supernatural factor, or whether it is nothing but an atavistic survival, an inherited ' Christian sickness ' barring the way towards the so-called moral (or unmoral) freedom.

After his failure in *Emperor and Galilean*, Ibsen is not quite sure of the answer to this vital question. He hesitates, as it were, between the natural and the metaphysical views, or rather, he avoids any definite explanation of the riddle, sheltering himself now in the ' Categorical Imperative,' now in the Darwinian theory of inheritance, or even in evasive subconscious phenomena (telepathy, suggestion, etc.). But be it as it may, in a certain stage of development we cannot reach either happiness or freedom without our moral sanction; for our ' sickly conscience' weighs us down like a 'corpse on our back,' paralysing the impetus of our will and even when our intellect passes this barrier, our will stumbles over it.

II

An excellent illustration of this is *Rosmersholm*. ' I know no Christian morality. I know no other morality than that I have within me,' states the ex-pastor Johannes Rosmer in

Ibsen's preliminary notes. He pretends to be free from all the 'ghosts,' and together with his spiritual emancipation grows his impulse towards happiness and joy. In the first draft of the drama he does not even intend to 'ennoble men.' He is craving only for the happiness of his personal life. Like one who has awakened from the dead he exclaims: 'All around, in every department of life, a luxuriant germinating is going on. And it is time that I too began to live. I must and will be happy in this world.'

'It is in the air. It is one of the greatest things about the new age that we dare openly proclaim happiness as our end in life,' adds Miss Dankett (later Rebecca West). But here the old-fashioned Gylling (later Rector Kroll) gives the ominous answer : 'Poor man, you with your conscience burdened with guilt—you think you can find happiness by those paths. . . . You are founding your happiness on water.'

A still more impressive warning is given by Hetman (later Ulrik Brendel) when he returns to Rosmer from his unsuccessful 'mission': 'It's all rubbish, my boy. Empty dreams. Nothing but mocking shadows that drag us down to destruction. Humanity is past help. . . . Because a mistake was made at the very Creation. . . . The Master deceived Himself, my boy. . . . The Master feels that there is a flaw in the work. And so he takes a firm stand. Insecurity of conscience, my boy. And that is what we have all inherited. That is why humanity is incurable. Past help.'

' Then is life worth living ? ' asks Rebecca.

' Oh, yes. Only avoid doing silly things. No quackery. Let life swing right or left—just as it chances.'

' But one's self ? Each individual ? '

' Eat, drink, and be merry, my fair young lady. And you must take existence in the same way, Rosmer. The Master forgot to give us wings. Both inner and outer ones. So let us crawl on the earth as long as we can. There is nothing else to be done.'

In the final version Ibsen naturally becomes more reserved on this delicate subject; and also more subtle—by transferring the psychological centre of gravity to Rebecca and complicating thereby the inner dilemma of Rosmer himself.

III

When Rebecca came to Rosmersholm she was ' beyond good and evil.' Her conscience was completely ' emancipated,' and therefore her indomitable will did not know any barriers. In order to attain her aim (Rosmer's love), she begins to ' emancipate ' him also, and by cunning combinations she brings his half-witted wife Beata to suicide. At last all the conditions for the fulfilment of her wishes are present, but here the real drama begins.

As for Johannes Rosmer, he is a descendant of stern puritans who have never laughed. At the same time, he is one of the most noble and absolutely moral characters created by Ibsen. But his very nobility is the cause of his weakness; he is naïve like a child, credulous, impractical, and irresolute. After having emancipated himself from the church, he suddenly decides to make all people round him noble and happy— ' to go as a messenger of emancipation from home to home; to win over minds and wills; to create noblemen in wider and wider circles. . . . Joyful noblemen. For it is joy that ennobles the mind. . . .' He wants to blend happiness and vocation for the sake of happiness. But he is paralysed in this task by his ' insecurity of conscience ' as soon as he begins to feel himself guilty of the death of his wife.

' I shall never get over this—wholly. There will always be a doubt—a question left. I can never again revel in that which makes life so marvellously sweet to live !' he complains to Rebecca.

' What is it you mean, Rosmer ? '

' Peaceful, happy innocence. . . .'

At last he sees but one means of getting over it—in marrying Rebecca. ' Then she (Beata) will be completely out of the saga—for ever and ever. . . . It must be so! It must! I cannot —I will not go through life with a corpse on my back. Help me to cast it off, Rebecca. And let us stifle all memories in freedom, in joy, in passion. You shall be to me the only wife I have ever had.'

And here, quite unexpectedly, Rebecca refuses his offer; she refuses it resolutely and almost with awe. For, in the meantime, she too has changed; her reckless will has come under the power of her awakened moral consciousness. After having voluntarily confessed her guilt in Beata's death, she discloses in a powerful scene the tragic history of the moral regeneration for which she has paid so dearly :—

' Rosmersholm has broken me. Broken me utterly and hopelessly. I had a fresh, untamed will when I came here. Now I have bent my neck under a strange law. . . . I believe I could have accomplished anything—at that time. For I had still my undaunted, free-born will. I

knew no scruples—I stood in awe of no human
relation. But then began what has broken down
my will, and cowed me so piteously for my whole
life. Rosmersholm has sapped my strength.
My old undaunted will has had its wings clipped
here. It is crippled! The time is passed when
I had courage for anything in the world. I
have lost the power of action, Rosmer. . . . It
is the Rosmer view of life that has infected my
will. And made me sick. Enslaved me to laws
that had no power over me before. You—life
with you—has ennobled my mind—you may
safely believe it! The Rosmer view of life
ennobles. But it kills happiness . . . Yes,
Rosmer, *this is* the terrible part of it: that now,
when all life's happiness is within my grasp—
my heart is changed and my own past cuts me
off from it. . . .'

Although happiness is within their reach, the
' strange law ' bars their way to it, demanding
retribution. As they do not believe in an eternal
Judge over them, they pass judgment upon
themselves. Their wedding feast is a voluntary
death in the same mill-race which once engulfed
the wife of Rosmer, deluded by Rebecca. 'The
dead wife has taken them.'

IV

To a further and still more complicated development of this dilemma Ibsen returns in the *Master-Builder*; but in the interval between *Rosmersholm* and this drama he wrote two other plays—*The Lady from the Sea* and *Hedda Gabler* —which deal rather with some special aspects of the problem of the individual will.

, As a matter of fact, in these two plays we encounter again a striking difference of mood for the very reason that in the sunny *Lady from the Sea* the well-intentioned ideologist reappears again (and for the last time) while in *Hedda Gabler* he entirely yields to the cold vivisector.

The *Lady from the Sea* represents a not entirely successful attempt to embody two themes. One of them is the ' dependence of our will on that which is will-less ' (Ellida's helpless longing for the Sea). But the second and the main theme of the play brings it partly into connection with Nora's and Mrs Alvings's dilemma—in so far as it is concerned with the relations between man' and wife. Ellida, who has ' sold ' herself to her husband, Doctor Wangel, cannot acclimatise herself to her new family and new surroundings, for

115

her will is permanently fascinated by the ' Unknown ' (symbolised by the enigmatic Stranger).
' I know you can keep me here,' she says to her
good-natured husband. ' You have the power,
and, no doubt, you will use it! But my mind—all
my thoughts—all my irresistible longings and
desires—these you cannot fetter! They will
yearn and strain—out into the Unknown—that
I was created for—and that you have barred
against me.'

Finally when the Stranger returns, the hour
of decision comes; she has to choose for ever
between him and her husband. Ellida wavers.
But as soon as she is free to decide on her own
responsibility, she is ' saved from herself,' and
the Unknown ceases to fascinate her. ' I was
free to choose it; therefore, I was able to reject
it. . . .' To her true liberation comes not
from outside but from within, and she ' acclima-
tises ' herself at last.

This is the ' positive ' crux of the play, which,
on the whole, produces the impression of a too
elaborated, too clever, and therefore not quite
convincing work.

Completely organic and convincing, however,
is Ibsen's next psychological play, *Hedda Gabler*,
in which the ideologist, as such, is reduced to
a minimum. In its chief character, Hedda, we

have the drama of the will without any direction,
'call,' or meaning. In her we feel great possibilities strangled by a small and vulgar existence.
She has ' no gift for anything but being bored,'
as Ibsen puts it in his preliminary notes. And,
again: 'Hedda's despair is that there are,
doubtless, so many chances in the world, but
she cannot discover them. It is the want of an
object in life that torments her.'

In the atmosphere of Bracks and Tesmans
her life resembles a dull journey, without aim or
end. And so her own potential strength (with its
cowardly yearning for beauty and life) becomes
destructive, and at last, turning against herself,
drives her to suicide.

After this drama of stagnation, Ibsen returned
to the drama of the creative will in *The Master-
Builder*, which is connected on the one side
with *Rosmersholm*,· and, on the other, with his
last three plays, especially *When We Dead Awaken*.

v

The old master-builder Solness is at a deadlock
with himself. He has succeeded in his ' call '
and vocation, but he has paid for success with
his happiness.

' All that I have succeeded in doing, building, creating—oh, isn't it terrible even to think of——! . . . That all this I have to make up for—not in money, but in human happiness. And not with my own happiness only, but with other people's too. That is the price which my position as an artist has cost me—and others. And every single day I have to look on while the price is paid for me anew. Over again, and over again—and over again for ever.'

Among his victims was not only the old Knut Brovik, but also his own wife Aline, who lost her two children in the burning of the very house on the ashes of which Solness started his brilliant career as architect. Solness pities his victims, yet cannot help crushing them. He seems to be the instrument, as it were, of some hidden power which acts through him; but he pays for the actions of this power—pays with the tortures of his conscience and a permanent fear of the inexorable retribution of the young generation which may crush him one day as he once crushed his own master, Knut Brovik. His success in building, he says, is like a sore on his breast. His mysterious helpers and servers flay other people so as to heal his wound. ' But still the sore is not healed—never, never !

Oh, if you knew how it can sometimes gnaw and burn.'

' I wonder whether you weren't sent into the world with a sickly conscience. . . . I mean that your conscience is feeble—too delicately built, as it were—hasn't strength to take a grip of things—to lift and bear what's heavy,' answers young Hilda Wangel, who comes like a fresh wind to his house to stir his doubting soul and reawaken it to its highest creative possibility.

When she was quite a young girl, Solness enchanted her mind by daring the ' impossible.' As she saw him high over the cheering crowd, she heard ' harps in the air,' and now she comes to Solness to see him again on his highest heights. She comes to the old master just at the moment when his inner division has reached its climax: when the ' sickly conscience ' weighs him down like a terrible burden and he begins to realise that, in spite of all his sacrifices, in spite of all his victims, nothing has been really built or is worth building.

Solness himself explains to Hilda that he once started his vocation as a true creator, as one who was chosen by God Himself. ' He (God) wanted to give me the chance of becoming an accomplished master in my own sphere—so that I might build all the more glorious churches

for Him. . . . Then I saw plainly why He had
taken my little children from me. It was that
I should have nothing else to attach myself to.
No such thing as love and happiness, you understand. I was to be only a master-builder—nothing
else. And all my life long I was to go on building
for Him. . . . First of all, I searched and tried
my own heart—then I did the impossible—I
no less than He. . . . I had never been able
to climb to a great, free height. But that day
I did it. . . . And when I stood there, high
over everything, and was hanging the wreath
over the vane, I said to Him: Hear me now,
Thou Mighty One! From this day forward
I will be a free builder—I, too, in my sphere—
just as Thou in Thine. I will never more build
any more churches for thee—only homes for
human beings. . . .'

But he soon came to the conclusion that this
utilitarian ' building homes for human beings
is not worth sixpence. . . . Yes, for now I see
it. Men have no use for these homes of theirs
—to be happy in. And I shouldn't have any
use for such a home, if I'd had one. . . .'
Greater things are necessary: dwelling-places
for a fuller human life—houses with high
church-towers that ' point up into the free air.
With the vane at a dizzy height.' He wants

to create ' castles in the air,' but on a firm foundation, thus attempting the reconciliation of his ' call ' with the greatest happiness and joy.

He has, in fact, built for himself a new home with a high tower. And now, inspired by Hilda, he decides to make new Life instead of new houses. Oblivious of his wife, Aline, to whom he is ' chained as to a dead woman,' oblivious of all his former victims, he wants to do the impossible again—he wants to ' climb as high as he builds.' And before his ascent he promises Hilda to speak again from his height to the Almighty. ' I will stand up there and talk to Him as I did that time before. . . . I will say to Him: Hear me, Mighty Lord—Thou mayst judge me as seems best to Thee. But thereafter I will build nothing but the loveliest thing in the world—build it together with a princess whom I love. . . . And then I will say to Him: Now I shall go down and throw my arms round her and kiss her—many, many times, I will say. . . . Then I will wave my hat—and come down to the earth and do as I said to Him.'

He actually puts the wreath on the top of the tower; he boldly speaks to the Mighty Lord, waves his hat, but here his ' dizzy conscience ' betrays him, and he crashes down from his height into the quarry.

The young Hilda exults, for she has heard again ' harps in the air '; but her master is dead.

So in the assertion of life through the organic union of the earthly and heavenly principles—of life as the highest, religious creation (so much more difficult and more important than the creation of art), Solness failed. On the one side, he was foiled by his ' sickly conscience,' and on the other, he erected his ' castle in the air ' in his own name, founding it on his self-will as creator for himself and for his own sake—not as one who fulfils his ' Master's Will.'

Therefore, he was not strong enough to bridge that abyss which separates our present consciousness from the new religious consciousness of the ' Third Empire.' His self-erected heights made him dizzy, and instead of victor he became victim.

CHAPTER IX
The 'Awakening of the Dead'

IX

THE 'AWAKENING OF THE DEAD'

I

IBSEN'S plays from *Brand* onwards show clearly how passionately he sought, even in his destructive criticism, for a synthetic way and value of life, and how each of his attempts in this direction ended in failure. He could not overcome his antitheses in a religious assertion of life with its all-embracing Sympathy ; nor could he find an issue in the opposite direction—an egotistic self-assertion and moral self-will—for he was not strong enough to cope with his 'sickly conscience.' He was therefore constantly struggling against the danger of remaining poised just over that neutral point where there is neither a complete assertion nor a complete negation, but only a paralysing scepticism. This struggle was Ibsen's most characteristic inner secret; and those who are able to grasp it may understand also the 'psychological' essence of his idealism, as well as the reason why his creation of Art never became creation of Life, but remained to the end only a stern criticism of life.

If, however, no synthetic reconciliation is possible between the impulse towards the ' call ' and the impulse towards 'life,' we must arrive sooner or later at a conscious battle between them, and in this conflict no value which uses life merely as a means to one's 'call' (moral or artistic) can stand successfully against the claims of life itself—'the beautiful, miraculous earth-life, the inscrutable earth-life' with all its attainable joy and happiness. A conscious 'transvaluation of values' on behalf of life and happiness invariably takes place. Or as one of Ibsen's characters (in the preliminary notes to *Rosmersholm*) exclaims: 'It is one of the greatest things about the new age that we dare openly proclaim happiness as our end in life.'

Until *Emperor and Galilean* we can see in Ibsen himself Brand's uncompromising struggle for his 'call.' But in the succeeding plays a gradually growing desire for happiness is perceptible. Nevertheless, he is fated, like his hero Rubek, to remain a creator and to sacrifice all joy and happiness to his vocation even against his own will. 'For I was born to be an artist, you see. And, do what I may, I shall never be anything else. . . . I have come to realise that

126

The 'Awakening of the Dead'

I am not at all adapted for seeking happiness and indolent enjoyment. Life does not shape itself that way for me and those like me. I must go on working—producing one work after another—right up to my dying day.'

Thus his vocation becomes a burden to him and a sin against life—in so far as he is compelled to make life only a means to his Art. It is not his fault that it is so, for he acts, as it were, under the spell of some inner Imperative, which is stronger than his will; yet he has to expiate his involuntary sin against life—expiate it in suffering and remorse. He pays for it in human happiness. 'And every single day I have to look on while the price is paid for me anew. Over again, and over again—and over again for ever. . . .' Finally, after his life-long creation and heroic struggle, we find him on the plinth of Rubek's symbolic statue among the human figures with dimly-suggested animal-faces: 'In front, beside a fountain sits a man weighed down with guilt, who cannot quite free himself from the earth-crust. I call him remorse for a forfeited life. He sits there and dips his fingers in the purling stream—to wash them clean—and he is gnawed and tortured by the thought that never, never will he succeed. Never in all eternity will he attain to freedom and the new life. He will remain for ever prisoned in his hell. . . .'

After a life sacrificed to his ' call ' the creator awakes only to see that in his struggle for the meaning and regeneration of iife he has lost life itself without having found a real compensation for the loss. When, severed from life, he reached his spiritual heights, they were empty and cold. In their ' great silence ' he found no real resurrection. The *Master-Builder* was the daring effort of a creator ' to climb as high as he builds '; but after the symbolic downfall of Solness there is no more daring: Ibsen's former warlike pathos is replaced by resignation and remorse. His last three plays—*Little Eyolf, John Gabriel Borkman,* and *When We Dead Awaken*—are a sufficient illustration. They are, in fact, dramas of awakening from the dead, dramas of the Last Judgment, but in no way dramas of Resurrection.

II

We saw, in the *Master-Builder,* Solness crushed in the moment of triumph because he had ascended his height in his own name, for the sake of his own egoistic happiness and will to power; in Allmers, the hero of *Little Eyolf* Ibsen tried, as it were, to correct the impetus of Solness by opposing to it (again on a solely moral plane) the other path—the path of self-denial and renunciation. But instead of the striving will of the tragic master-builder, we find in Alfred Allmers only an exhausted moral will.

This tender, brooding, and rather passive character was writing a big book on Human Responsibility which was to have been his life-work. But in the great solitude of the mountains a sudden change came over him: he became aware that in writing he was wasting his time and powers; so he returned home—to act out his ' human responsibility ' in life, realising that without the ' joy of self-sacrifice ' all his creation was mere egoism. ' I have been too much taken up by myself and by—by all these morbid, distorted, baseless fancies that I, myself, had some special mission in the world. Something of extreme importance and moment—something that concerned myself alone,' he states (in the preliminary notes of the drama). And so he decides to efface himself and to devote all his forces to his little son Eyolf, who fell from a table and was crippled for life at a moment when Allmers and his sensual wife, Rita, were indulging in wild passion. He wants to develop all the rich possibilities of that young soul in order to ' create a conscious happiness in his mind.' But while the passionate Rita is demanding all the affection of Allmers for herself, unwilling to share it even with her own child, the little Eyolf, spellbound, follows the enigmatic Rat-wife down to the pier and is drowned.

The whole inner drama of Rita and Alfred Allmers now turns round this catastrophe. To Alfred the punishment seems unjust and senseless; since Eyolf himself has committed no crime, there is no need of his death in retribution or atonement. ' The whole thing is utterly groundless and meaningless. And yet the order of the world requires it.'

In their brooding self-reproach the parents discover that both of them have been egoists towards Eyolf since his birth; they condemned their child in that very moment of sensual indulgence when they left him unwatched on the table. And Rita makes the subtle and very true remark that even Alfred's sudden decision to devote all his life to his crippled son is nothing but an act of disguised egoism. ' Because you had begun to doubt whether you had any great vocation to live for in the world. And then you needed something new to fill up your life.' In other words, their son was always only a ' little stranger boy' among them. 'And so, after all, there was retribution in Eyolf's death. . . . Judgment upon you and me. . . . And now, what we now call sorrow and heartache—is really the gnawing of conscience, Rita. Nothing else.'

Like Rosmer and Rebecca, they do not believe in an eternal Judge, and yet they too bend under the 'strange law.' In doing this, they see a meaning in the catastrophe, as well as in their atonement; their profound suffering purifies and ennobles them, but they pay a terrible price for their ennobling—they pay with 'the loss of all, all life's happiness.' Although regenerated, they have 'nothing to fill life with. An empty void on all sides—wherever I look. . . .'

At last, they find 'something that is a little like love' in their philanthropic decision to educate the very children who did not save Eyolf, although they could have done so. This step is, however, only a mask for their resignation; in spite of their looking 'upwards, towards the stars and the great silence,' their sudden philanthropy is but an escape from the impending void of their lives—a subterfuge in which they hope to find 'something that would counterbalance the loss of happiness,' as Ibsen puts it in the preliminary notes. 'Nothing that would equal happiness. But something that might make life liveable'; for they are so earth-bound, that they want to live their life at any price and 'in spite of all.'

It is not wonderful that in this play we do not hear the triumphant song of a real new life; the moral regeneration of Allmers and Rita is at the same time a loss of life and a final capitulation before it. Especially towards the end of the drama we are too conscious of the melancholy motive of Allmers's still 'fellow-traveller' in the mountains—the motive of Death. And this motive becomes dominant in Ibsen's next work, *John Gabriel Borkman*, from every page of which is heard the gloomy rhythm of the *Danse Macabre*.

III

John Gabriel Borkman had, like Solness, his life-call. He wanted to conquer what he regarded as his own kingdom—the buried spirits of the mines. 'I felt the irresistible vocation within me! The imprisoned millions lay all over the country, deep in the bowels of the earth, calling aloud to me! They shrieked to me to free them. But no one else heard their cry—I alone had ears for it. . . . I wanted to have at my command all the sources of power in this country. All the wealth that lay hidden in the soil, and the rocks, and the forests, and the sea—I wanted to gather it all in my hands, to make myself master of it all, and so to promote the well-being of many, many thousands.'

But for the sake of this irresistible vocation he committed the crime ' for which there is no forgiveness,' the crime against the living life; he killed the happiness and the love-life in a beloved and loving woman by using her simply as a means to his vocation. ' What you held dearest in the world you were ready to barter away for gain,' she reproaches him many years later. ' That is the double crime you have committed! The murder on your soul and on mine. . . . You have done to death all the gladness of life in me. . . .'

So the theme of this drama is only a new and subtle modification of the dilemma which we find in Brand, Julian, Rosmer, and Solness. The financier Borkman was of a harder metal than Rosmer or Solness; but in his love and longing for power he transgressed the worldly law and became a social outcast. Rejected, forgotten, he walked for years like a ' sick wolf,' up and down the room in which he was buried alive. But when the woman whom he once had loved and sold suddenly visits him, he awakens for a moment from the dead: ' I have been close to the verge of death. But now I have awakened. I have come to myself. A whole life lies before me yet. I can see it awaiting me, radiant and quickening. And you—you shall see it, too.'

' Never dream of life again! Lie quiet where you are,' cruelly replies his wife, who has been preparing a splendid living ' monument' over his grave. This monument is her son Erhart, whose ' mission' it is to restore the family name, so polluted by the lapse of his father. ' His life shall be so pure and high and bright, that your burrowing in the dark shall be as though it had never been!'

Erhart, however, does not trouble very much about ' missions' and ' vocations.' The only thing he cares for is happiness, or what he understands as happiness. ' I am young! That is what I never realised before; but now the knowledge is tingling through every vein in my body. I will not work! I will only live, live, live. For happiness, mother!' . . . And he illustrates his philosophy of life with sufficient eloquence by running away from all those living dead to the bright South with a certain Mrs Wilton, who also wants happiness and nothing less. But while these two are hurrying

134

towards their somewhat problematic happiness, the old Borkman suddenly decides to rise to life —to work out his own redemption by beginning at the bottom again. After several years of seclusion in his stifling grave he now rushes out into the winter-night, 'out into the storm of life.' Ella, the beloved woman of his young days, follows him, and from the hill they look again together upon all the dreams of their youth, now buried for ever in snow and darkness. The raving Borkman listens anew to the magic call of his imprisoned millions; he listens to all the familiar voices coming from his vast, infinite kingdom and whispers: 'I love you, unborn treasures yearning for the light! I love you, love you, love you. . . .'

'Yes, your love is still down there, John. But here, in the light of day, here there was a living, warm, human heart that throbbed and glowed for you. And this heart you crushed. Oh, worse than that! Ten times worse! You sold it. . . . And therefore, I prophesy to you, John Gabriel Borkman—you will never enter in triumph into your cold, dark kingdom!'

And, in fact, no sooner did Ella utter her prophecy than a 'hand of ice' clutched at his heart and killed him. He awoke from the dead only to see that he had died long before his death and that there was no resurrection. This was the retribution for his heavy sin against Life.

IV

We encounter a variation of the same theme in the dramatic Epilogue, *When We Dead Awaken*, which represents Ibsen's final sentence upon himself and his artistic creation. The sculptor Rubek in whom the conflict between the ' call ' and happiness once more reaches its highest pitch, committed, like Borkman, a great sin against Life: he placed 'the dead clay-image above the happiness of life—of love.'

After having ' lightly and carelessly taken a warm-blooded body, a young human life, and worn the soul out of it '—because he needed it for his work of art, he became rich and famous; his statue called ' Resurrection Day ' spread the name of its creator all over the world, and the price paid for that was the ardent soul of his young model Irene, whose love he left unanswered—from ' higher motives.'

' I came to look on you as a thing hallowed, not to be touched save in adoring thoughts. In those days I was still young, Irene. And the superstition took hold of me that if I touched you, if I desired you with my senses, my soul would be profaned, so that I should be unable to accomplish what I was striving for. I still think there was some truth in that,' he confesses to Irene many years later, when he meets her in the mountains.

' The work of art first—then the human being,' scornfully answers Irene. ' I was a human being then! And I, too, had a life to live—and a human destiny to fulfil! And all that I let slip—gave it all up in order to make myself your bondswoman. Oh, it was self-murder—a deadly sin against myself! And that sin I can never expiate. . . . I ought never to have served you—poet! '

Her ' self-murder ' left her empty and soulless. But Rubek, too, created nothing great after her sudden disappearance—nothing except busts of respectable plutocrats with pompous animals' faces behind the masks. ' I no longer loved my work. Men's laurels and incense nauseated me, till I could have rushed away in despair and hidden myself in the depths of the woods. . . . All the talk about the artists' missions and so forth, began to strike me as being very empty and hollow, and meaningless at bottom.'

' Then what would you put in its place ? ' asks Maia.

' Life, Maia. . . .'

Like Solness he wanted to replace Art by Life,
the life of beauty, sunshine, and happiness, which
he had let slip for the sake of his vocation. He
awoke from the dead. But while he was able
to symbolise Resurrection in a magnificent statue,
he could not achieve it in his own life. After
having condemned his artistic past, he sets out
with Irene on an ascent to the mountain-summits,
without suspecting that presently they ' may
come to a tight place where you can neither get
forward nor back. And then you stick fast,
Professor! Mountain-fast, we hunters call it. . . .'
In spite of Ulfheim's warning, they are firm in
their decision. But while approaching the
heights of their new life, they perceive suddenly
and ultimately that they are not two living
beings, only two dead ' clay-cold bodies,' playing
with each other.

' The love that belongs to the life of earth—
the beautiful, miraculous earth-life—the inscrutable earth-life—that is dead in both of us. . . .
The desire for life is dead in me, Arnold. Now
I have arisen. And I look for you. And
then I see that you and life lie dead—as I
have lain. . . . The young woman of your
Resurrection Day can see all life lying on
its bier. . . .'

The 'Awakening of the Dead'

They awaken from the dead in order to see, not only that they never have lived, but also that for them there is no life at all—neither in their cold heights, nor in Ulfheim's lower regions of 'indolent enjoyments' where Maia sings her song of freedom. The only thing that remains is a conscious illusion which is the most terrible of all illusions. 'Then let two of the dead—us two—for once live life to its uttermost—before we go down to our graves again!' exclaims Rubek in his despair, throwing his arms round Irene.

But even that is not granted them; while they try to reach through the mist 'the summit of the tower that shines in the sunrise,' an avalanche buries them. Here the Sister of Mercy —all in black—appears, makes the sign of the Cross over them and whispers: ' *Pax vobiscum!* '

These are the last symbolic words of Ibsen. And, indeed, what, or about what, could he have written after this play which in itself gives the impression of a 'tight place where you can neither get forward nor back. And then you stick fast. . . .' It was Ibsen's last attempt to overcome his inner dilemma, and, at the same time, his last and final defeat.

CHAPTER X

Conclusion

X

In concluding the present study of Ibsen and his work, it is hardly necessary to emphasise the fact that he is one of those few writers who are eminently contemporary, chiefly because their personal inner drama (in so far as they manifest it in their works) is like a searchlight illuminating and revealing the spiritual undercurrents of modern individuality. By means of this searchlight we can lay bare some of the most characteristic features of contemporary man and of his inner cul-de-sac.

Ibsen is, indeed, the poet of this cul-de-sac. In the drama of his consciousness, in his struggle with paralysing scepticism, in his vain striving for a real creative value, he is so near us that he might be taken as a symbol of our own 'split,' longing and impotent selves.

It is true his mind was much more acute than profound; his lead touched but a comparatively small area of that spiritual underworld, the labyrinths of which were so familiar to another great seeker, Dostoevsky. Ibsen even gives the impression of being strong and intense for the very reason that he is somewhat one-sided and narrow. This narrowness, however, is due to his eye being directed not so much towards the depths as towards the heights of the human soul ; nor must one forget that he was far more the fastidious aristocrat in his creation than Dostoevsky; and it was perhaps this aristocratic instinct that prevented his entering those dark apocalyptic depths of the human soul which were the favourite area of the great Russian writer.

On the other hand, it is largely due to a certain restriction of his creative sphere that he revealed to us so strikingly the heroic and tragic potency within the modern (*i.e.* most unheroic) individual even within the modern average man. Moreover, Ibsen's art—up to his last dramas of resignation—shows, on the whole, not so much a pessimistic as a tragic attitude towards man and life.

To make clear this difference it may be well to point out that the pessimistic attitude is merely negative, and therefore uncreative, while the tragic attitude is an overcoming of pessimism through pessimism itself. A tragic individual approaches life, not through a ready-made optimism or sentimental idealism, but by bravely facing our existence in its most negative aspects, and consciously striving to transform it just because of its vulgarity and evil. This attitude is beyond sterile pessimism, as it is beyond that naïve and sheltered optimism which sees in reality only what it wishes to see. It is perhaps the only attitude that leads to a creative transvaluation and transformation of life.

In order to achieve such a transvaluation, two things are essential; the first is a robust creative will, and the second is an over-individual Value in the name of which one must strive. Without a value of this kind the struggle is in danger of becoming a mere struggle for struggle's sake, and the conquered inner freedom nothing but a freedom for the sake of freedom.

Thus we come to the most salient feature of Ibsen's mentality : he had an intense creative will without an adequate creative Value. And what is still more striking, he failed to reach this value chiefly because of his exaggerated moral consciousness—in so far as this was 'autonomous,' *i.e.* differentiated from, or rather devoid of, religious consciousness.

We have seen the gradual process of this failure, which in itself goes to prove the insufficiency and sterility of our present mental plane. Ibsen's work, as a 'psychological' whole, is an unremitting and unsuccessful endeavour to transcend this plane. At the same time, it stands as a tragic record of an age in which all the past inner values have been lived out, while new ones are yet unborn.